49 Days Back to Better

Advance Praise for
49 Days Back to Better

"Never in my life have I needed God's word to help me make decisions and to change my own behavior and lead others in my organization than in the weeks since COVID-19 hit the U.S. Studying the *49 Days Back to Better* devotional provided inspiration for decisions as life was changing and reshaping in front of my eyes. Without scripture, I could not have met the challenge of this unprecedented time."

—**Judy Long,** president and chief operating officer,
First Citizens National Bank

"You were created to make a positive difference in the world around you! This *49 Days Back to Better* devotional is a great resource to help you discover or re-discover your purpose in life and accomplish everything God has planned for you!"

—**Jason Crabb,** multi-Grammy-winning artist

"*49 Days Back to Better* is more than a devotional. It's more like 49 days of self-awareness. This is an easy read that is practical and very relational. Every day will have you thinking and looking at things deeper."

—**Heather Adams,** multi-unit Chick-fil-A owner/operator,
Huntsville, Alabama

"*49 Days Back to Better* can help you think deeply about the purpose God has given you in life and how you can live it to its fullest! You could be 49 days away from something special!"

—**Jerry Reese,** two-time Super Bowl champion,
former general manager of the New York Giants

"Dr. Tim Hill and Tim Enochs have crafted a devotional that is easy to use, yet impactful in its application. You'll use it every day!"

—**Barry Landis,** executive director, The Briner Institute
and chairman of Ribbow Media Group

"God wants us to discover the purpose and plans He has for us. He wants us to ask, and He wants to reveal those plans. Sometimes He gives us just enough light to see the next step we need to take, and other times He gives us a bold vision with greater clarity of what He has in store. In *49 Days Back to Better,* my friend Tim Enochs, and Dr. Tim Hill continue to use their gifts to help others discover and live out their purpose. This devotional can help all of us discover the plans God has for us and find the part we play in God's Kingdom."

—**Greg Bays,** vice president, Integrity Music

"*49 Days Back To Better* is 49 days of teaching, or perhaps reminding ourselves, about what is truly important in our lives. Now, more than ever, we need to focus on what really matters in our lives and how it impacts those around us!"

—**Tricia Allison,** Mother of five children, Wife,
Regional Manager, Supreme Lending

49 Days Back to ~~Normal~~ *Better*

Change Your Trajectory
for a New Outlook on Life

Dr. Tim Hill
Tim Enochs
with Adam Enochs

NASHVILLE

NEW YORK • LONDON • MELBOURNE • VANCOUVER

49 Days Back to Better

Change Your Trajectory for a New Outlook on Life

Published in New York, New York, by Morgan James Publishing. Morgan James is a trademark of Morgan James, LLC. www.MorganJamesPublishing.com

Proudly distributed by Ingram Publisher Services.

A **FREE** ebook edition is available for you
or a friend with the purchase of this print book.

CLEARLY SIGN YOUR NAME ABOVE

Instructions to claim your free ebook edition:
1. Visit MorganJamesBOGO.com
2. Sign your name CLEARLY in the space above
3. Complete the form and submit a photo
   of this entire page
4. You or your friend can download the ebook
   to your preferred device

ISBN 9781631957185 paperback
ISBN 9781631957192 ebook
Library of Congress Control Number:
2021943234

Cover Design by:
Rachel Lopez
www.r2cdesign.com

Interior Design by:
Christopher Kirk
www.GFSstudio.com

with...

Morgan James is a proud partner of Habitat for Humanity Peninsula
and Greater Williamsburg. Partners in building since 2006.

Get involved today! Visit MorganJamesPublishing.com/giving-back

To everyone who has lost a family member, a friend, co-worker, job, or anything else, including hope, during this pandemic.

While we can't go back to normal, we can help each other go back to something better than what current circumstances seem to offer.

Table of Contents

Foreword

My friend, and general overseer of the Church of God, Dr. Tim Hill, and *New York Times* best-selling author, executive coach, and founder of NEWLife Leadership, Tim Enochs, have written a dynamic devotional which will carry you through *49 Days Back to Better*. As we make our way back from this worldwide pandemic, you don't have to go back to normal. You can go back to better. God has given you a roadmap to success which goes far beyond any level of earthly success you might imagine.

In the world's eyes, success may be measured by many standards which don't last. Consider this, in Matthew 16:26 we read: *For what profit is it to a man if he gains the whole world, and loses his own soul? Or what will a man give in exchange for his soul?* Many people have given up what matters most in their life, chasing the world's definition of success. Relationships have been destroyed, physical and emotional health have been devastated, and many have become miserable chasing the bright lights of what they thought defined success. That kind of success is completely and undeniably refutable. But it doesn't have to be that way for you! There is a better and brighter way!

Some people chase success measured by standards which don't last. Some are frozen by fear or a faulty belief system that won't allow them to "go for it" in life and work. They miss out on the joy of accomplishing what God has called and gifted them to do. In my book, *Limitless*, I wrote about how the devil will *try to put limits on your life with a spirit of lack . . . just as soon as you lift up your head and determine to go to the next level with God, that old deceiving spirit of lack will show up and try to hold you back.* Don't let that happen! This forty-nine-day journey to Back to Better can help.

God has called you to a higher level of success than many in this world can see or understand. It cannot be denied or disproven. It is a level of success that spills into the lives of everyone it touches. It can have uncommon influence on everyone around you by changing the trajectory of your life and theirs. You might say, it's contagious . . . in a good way. In Ephesians 2:10 (NLT) we read: *For we are God's masterpiece. He has created us anew in Christ Jesus, so we can do the good things He planned for us long ago.* You see, God has called you to complete work He ordained long ago for you to do. It's when you accomplish the aim or purpose for what He has called and gifted you to do that your success becomes irrefutable in this world and into eternity.

God's word says: *But on the judgment day, fire will reveal what kind of work each builder has done. The fire will show if a person's work has any value* (1 Cor. 3:13, NLT). The world can't disprove it, the enemy can't deny it, and the fire of testing won't burn it up. It's true, it's real, and it stands for eternity.

It's what Joshua wrote about in Joshua 1:8 when he said you would have *good success.* It's what Solomon wrote in Proverbs 16:3 (NLT) when he said: *commit to the Lord whatever you do, and your plans would succeed* and in Proverbs 3:4 (ESV), *So you will find favor and good success in the sight of God and man.* It's the ultimate result of Psalm 37:4 (ESV) where David wrote: *Delight yourself in the Lord and He will give you the desires of your heart.* It's the outcome of what James was referring to when he said: *Humble yourselves before the Lord and He will exalt you* (James 4:10, ESV).

The door of opportunity is open for you to go back to better. Are you ready?

Take this forty-nine-day journey with me. By the power and ordained will of God, you and I can accomplish everything God wants us to accomplish so we will have something to lay at the feet of Jesus when we enter into the joys of the Lord. This is what it means to be a good and faithful servant.

Jentezen Franklin,
pastor and *New York Times* best-selling author

Preface

I t seems much of what we thought was normal about life and the world around us has changed. A tiny virus we can't see has shut down businesses, crippled nations, and taken the lives of precious people. Those lives can never be replaced. And then there is the petty stuff like finding a single roll of toilet paper at the supermarket.

We are wearing masks and gloves to protect ourselves and others from this unseen enemy potentially hiding inside our friends, neighbors, and possibly in members of our own family. Normal just isn't normal anymore. Normal is just a place in our minds that we all seem to want to get back to as soon as possible. Some people are even calling it a new normal, but what is that?

We've decided to take a different path. We've decided, in areas where we have a choice, we don't want to go back to someone else's definition of normal. We've decided we want to go back to better.

For those of you who have lost loved ones or friends, we are praying for you. As we consider the concept of *going back to better*, we fully understand that some losses can never be replaced, and in that realm, there is no going back to better. In this book, we are focused on areas where we have a choice whether to go back to normal in those areas or finding our way back to something better.

Going back to better in those areas means we are not going to just ride this thing out, hoping to limp our way back to normal. Here's how we see it. No matter what we have had to deal with, we are all going back to one of two futures . . .

1. A future where we are just along for the ride on our way to what the world defines as normal—or—
2. A future where we want to be more, do more, and give more than ever before. That's the future we want.

We want to help as many people as possible to discover, re-discover, or refine their purpose in life and create a clear/compelling plan of action to make it happen.

We didn't choose to invite this pandemic into our lives, but we want to make the best choices we can going forward. With God's help, we can!

Day 1
You Are on a Mission from God

For we are His workmanship, created in Christ Jesus
for good works, which God prepared beforehand
that we should walk in them.
Ephesians 2:10

When I (Tim Hill) was seven years old, I was sitting between my mom and dad in the back of the Texas Church of God tabernacle in Weatherford, TX in a camp meeting on a Sunday night. I had just started singing a little bit at my dad's church in Fort Worth. Someone in leadership had heard about it and had the idea to have me sing that night. The man in charge of the music came back to the back of that auditorium. He picked me up from between my parents, raced me down to the stage. He pulled a piano bench out. He stood me on top of it, put a microphone in front of my face and said: "Sing, boy." There I was, seven years old, standing on top of a piano bench in front of 800 people on a Sunday night, about to sing.

The only thing I could think to sing was a song my mom had been playing over and over on the old record player back at home . . . *I Wouldn't Take Nothing For My Journey Now.* I had no idea when I went to church that night, I would be singing in front of 800 people. That was a first step in a long journey of ministry for me. We are all on a mission from God.

We are all on a journey. While it has been difficult over the past several months and we don't know for sure what the future holds, we do know Who holds the future. It's been painful and we have shared the loss of loved ones and many things we once took for granted. Our hope must be in the One who called us and that He will help us go back to a future that is better than it may seem to be at this current moment in time. The only place we can start is where we are, and our hope must be that somehow, some way, God will show us the way.

What does "better" look like from where you are now? No matter what you have been through, good or bad, today is a different day. It's a fresh start and His mercies are new!

Through the Lord's mercies we are not consumed,
Because His compassions fail not.
They are new every morning; Great is Your faithfulness
Lamentations 3:22–23.

The past is the past and today is new. His mercies are new and today can be a fresh start on the road back to better. While defining better can be difficult, it isn't impossible . . . neither is it impossible to go back to better. Going back to better has three requirements:

1. Know you have a purpose in life.
2. Know your own personal purpose.

3. Take action to fulfill your purpose.

You have purpose in your life. Let's begin with discovering your personal purpose.

What is the purpose of your life? How much have you thought about that lately?

Do you have it written somewhere that you can read it at least weekly? You should!

Why are you here? Not here reading this book, but why are you here on earth?

Consider what God has to say about the topic . . . He created you in Christ Jesus for good works which He has already prepared for you to do. You know what that means? God has a plan for your life and good works for you to accomplish. Think about that for a minute . . . God, the one Who created everything, created you for a purpose! *Beforehand*, God created good works for you to accomplish.

God made you and equipped you for a purpose. Can you imagine the good works He has planned for you to accomplish? He already had them on His mind when He made you. You are not an accident. God has already set you up for these good works. You don't have to hope you have a purpose in life. God made you on purpose for a purpose.

Have you ever heard someone say: *I am on a mission from God!*

That's you! You can say that all day, every day. You are on a mission from God!

He has special work for you to do, and He set you up to be able to do it. The only way you can fail is if you don't lean into it and do your part.

Prayer

Heavenly Father, thank you for creating me for good works that you pre-planned for me to accomplish. Help me to understand what you want me to do and help me to live my purpose in life with every ounce of strength that you give me.

Think/Act

Think about good works you have already done in your life. This isn't bragging. Give God glory for each one. It is He who gave you the strength and opportunity. Make a list of these somewhere, and then write a short prayer of thanks to God and commitment to do more with His help.

_____

_____

_____

_____

_____

_____

_____

_____

_____

_____

_____

_____

_____

_____

_____

_____

_____

_____

_____

_____

_____

_____

_____

_____

_____

Day 2
A Simple Life

Make it your goal to live a quiet life.
1 Thessalonians 4:11 (NLT)

A dad surprised his son, who was twenty-four at the time, by taking him to a barber shop to get a straight razor shave. He had a shave like that a couple of years previously and knew that his son was in for the closest shave of his life (in a good way).

The barber gave him the works—pre-shave oil, shaving cream lathered and applied with a brush, and then the shave with an old-school straight razor. He was meticulous in the art of shaving. The dad watched every move to see how it was done. He just wasn't convinced he could use a straight razor on himself, or anyone else for that matter!

Then, just when he thought the shave was finished, the barber grabbed something that was very familiar to the dad: a Gillette Fusion razor. What could that be used for?

What his son and he discovered was the secret to a really close shave was actually no secret at all. It was found in the simple Gillette razor that the dad was already using every time he shaved.

The shave was a very cool experience for his son, and he was glad he planned for him to have that experience. However, he discovered that in many cases, the simple things can be the best things in life. The dad now has a newfound appreciation for his razor and a simple life.

Prayer

Heavenly Father, help me see where I am making life too complicated. Help me find ways to enjoy a simpler life, and help others do the same.

Think/Act

Take a look at your life and consider at least one simple thing that you already do to make your life better. Would you be willing to share that with others?

_____

_____

_____

_____

_____

_____

_____

_____

Day 3
Is Your Life Upside Down?

For as the heavens are higher than the earth, So are My ways
higher than your ways, And My thoughts than your thoughts.
Isaiah 55:9

Consider this riddle:

Look at me when I'm upside down and you'll be right side up . . .
Look at me when I'm right side up and you'll be upside down . . .
What am I?

A spoon.

You see, when you look at a spoon right side up (as it lies on a table) you will see your reflection upside down. But when you turn the spoon over and look at it, you see yourself right side up.

The mystery of this can be explained by physics. When it is right side up, a spoon is concave. Light naturally travels in a straight path and is therefore flipped on the concave side of a spoon . . . so you see yourself upside down.

If you further consider the shape of your eyes, they are also concave . . . so every image must be flipped. Our amazing brains perform this service for us automatically. So, if you think about it, in the case of looking at the concave side of a spoon, there is a double flip of the image.

Our lives can often seem overwhelming and complicated, to the extent that everything seems to be crashing in around us. If that is the case for you right now, maybe you just need a change of perspective.

Sometimes, just by looking at the same thing a different way, everything can change within your mind. That which seems complicated, impossible, or upside down can appear quite different when your perspective is flipped.

The situation hasn't changed, but your attitude and your response to the situation may be the complete opposite.

Sometimes in life, it's all about how you look at things. God's perspective is always perfect. Sometimes our perspective can be upside down.

Prayer

Heavenly Father help me to see Your perspective on the pressing aspects of my life today.

Think/Act

Try this science experiment for yourself. Look at your reflection on both sides of a spoon. (Of course, you know not to try this with a plastic spoon.) What's the difference? Your reflection is right side up one way and upside down the other. A simple flip of the spoon changes everything. Then, consider difficult situations in your life and try to find a different perspective. Consider where you have opportunities in those situations that you haven't considered before now and decide what to do next. That simple flip of perspective could change everything!

_____

_____

_____

_____

_____

_____

_____

_____

_____

_____

_____

_____

_____

_____

_____

Day 4

Your Thoughts Matter

. . . think on these things.
Philippians 4:8

The large assembly hall known as the Municipal Auditorium in Birmingham, Alabama, was filled to capacity on Saturday evening, August 28, 1948. The 42nd General Assembly of the Church of God began and was led in prayer by General Overseer, John C. Jernigan.

The 42nd General Assembly is best known as the one when the Declaration of Faith for the Church of God was written and adopted. It stood the test of time and has not been changed since being adopted.

However, while the writing and adoption of the Declaration of Faith was monumental, it was not the only significant event which happened during that time in Birmingham. Tuesday, August 31, was the final day of General Assembly and there was one final message to be delivered to the ministers by J. A. Self. His message was short but powerful. His message centered on the power of your thoughts.

He opened with one simple, yet impactful, verse from scripture:

> *Finally, brethren, whatsoever things are true,*
> *whatsoever things are honest, whatsoever things are just,*
> *whatsoever things are pure, whatsoever things are lovely,*
> *whatsoever things are of good report, if there be any virtue,*
> *and if there be any praise, THINK ON THESE THINGS.*
> Philippians 4:8 (emphasis ours)

J. A. Self said:

> Changing our thinking has much to do with our Christian living. The man who thinks right will come very near living right. If he thinks wrong, he is apt to go wrong. If he is careless in his thought life, he will find himself leaning to his own understanding and will make a sad mistake . . . The weapons of our warfare are not carnal.

He concluded with Philippians 4:9: *Those things, which ye have both learned, and received, and heard, and seen in me, do: and the God of peace shall be with you.*

In essence, what you think matters . . . it can affect every aspect of your life. Think on good things.

Prayer

Heavenly Father, I understand that what I think is important and I know Your word teaches me how to think. I need Your help to help me think on good things. Please help me center my thoughts on You and how Your word says I should be thinking.

Think/Act

What is the opposite of thinking on good things? Let's call it *stinking thinking*. Make a list of areas you believe you are thinking on good things and a list of areas where you may be experiencing *stinking thinking*. What's the difference? Why are you thinking good thoughts in some areas and have *stinking thinking* in others? How can you increase the areas of good thinking?

_____

_____

_____

_____

_____

_____

_____

_____

_____

_____

_____

Day 5

Time for an Attitude Check

I do not understand what I do.
For what I want to do I do not do, but what I hate I do.
Romans 7:15 (NIV)

*E*verything you do begins with a thought.

It has been said that your attitude is created by your thoughts.

Last week I had the pleasure of watching an intramural flag football team win an exciting game in overtime. But it was something that happened after the game that really grabbed my attention.

During the game, one of the players accidently cleated a player on the opposing team. He was wearing metal cleats. The accident didn't cause much of an altercation at the time . . . but then the injured player's team was defeated.

Immediately, the slightly injured player on the losing team ran up to the guy who had been wearing the metal cleats and yelled, "DON'T YOU EVER WEAR METAL CLEATS TO A GAME LIKE THIS AGAIN!" He pushed the guy backwards until his team pulled him away. From all appearances, he was looking for a fight.

The coach apologized to the player who had been pushed. He acknowledged that his player should apologize.

A few minutes later, the injured player made his apology. It went something like this: "I blew up and got mad. I have an anger problem and can't control myself sometimes. I'm sorry . . . but I could have broken every bone in your body if I had wanted to."

The other player was stunned.

He had already changed out of the metal cleats, apologized to the injured player, to the referees, and to the coach of the other team. In his mind, the matter had already been resolved.

However, the guy with the "anger problem" could see only one way to find resolution when the game was over . . . a fight.

Later, it struck me that the player who claimed he could not control his anger had in fact kept it under wraps from the time of the accident, throughout the balance of the game. He waited until after the game—more importantly, after his team lost—to blow up.

At first it was easy for me to judge that player and proclaim that, rather than an anger problem, he had an attitude problem. The truth is that we are all prone to attitude problems. It's how we choose to handle those situations that makes all the difference.

Have you checked your attitude lately?

Consider this: Stephen Covey, author of *The 7 Habits of Highly Effective People*, mentioned a space in time between stimulus and response over which we have total control. It's the time between when you are stimulated to do something and when you actually take action. That space in time may only be a millisecond, but it is still within your control.

Prayer

Heavenly Father, I know my thoughts come before every action I take. Help me to have the right attitude in everything, even before I say a word or take an action.

Think/Act

Over the next couple of weeks, try to pause and catch yourself reacting before you think. Journal what you've learned. It's easy to ignore that tiny space between stimulus and response. Remember, that space in time belongs to you. Use it well.

_____

_____

_____

_____

_____

_____

_____

_____

_____

_____

_____

_____

Day 6

Wishers, Talkers, Dreamers, Dabblers, and Doers

But be doers of the word, and not hearers only,
deceiving yourselves.
James 1:22 (KJV)

You may have heard it said that if you want something done, you should ask someone who is already busy. So, what are all the other people doing?

The easy answer is: not much.

Most of us have been guilty of operating out of one of these zones:

Wishers can often be found sighing wistfully, "I wish I may, I wish I might . . ." The problem is that Wishers never get up and make good things happen.

Talkers are full of big ideas they'd love to tell you about . . . but it turns out it's just hot air. All the talking in the world never gets things done.

Dreamers have big ideas, but they soon get distracted chasing the next big idea. Dreams are great . . . you should dream and dream big, but if you don't wake up and take action, your dreams will never come true.

Dabblers are interesting people. They are all about action, because they are always doing something. The problem is that they are too quickly bored or frustrated, so they move on and start dabbling in something else. As my dad used to say, "When a task is once begun, never leave it until it's done. Though the labor be great or small, do it well or not at all." His mom taught him that.

Doers are the people who actually get things done.

What may have started as a wish or a dream gets translated into a plan of action. What was once only talked about gets done. Rather than dabble in a lot of things, only the few most critical tasks are seen through to fruition.

Are you stuck in one of the first four zones? Is there something that you only wish for, talk about, dream of, or dabble in?

Make a commitment to do something today. Be a Doer!

Prayer

Heavenly Father, please help me to be more than a wisher, talker, dreamer, and dabbler. Please help me to do what you want me to do. Help me to do what it will take to be in the best position for my dreams and goals to come to fruition.

Think/Act

Make a list of the top 5 things you need to quit talking about but need to do. Add a "By When" date for when you will take that action. Then ask a family member or friend to hold you accountable to doing what you said you will do by the day you committed.

Note: The idea for Wishers, Talkers, Dreamers, Dabblers, and Doers is taken from a 2006 sermon by James May.

_____

_____

_____

_____

_____

_____

_____

_____

_____

_____

_____

_____

_____

_____

_____

_____

_____

_____

Day 7

I Can, and I Will

*But what do you think? A man had two sons, and he came
to the first and said, 'Son, go, work today in my vineyard.'
He answered and said, 'I will not,' but afterward he
regretted it and went. Then he came to the second and said
likewise. And he answered and said, 'I go, sir,' but he did
not go. Which of the two did the will of his father?*
Matthew 21:28–30a

I can—AND—I will.

Both proclamations are powerful, faith-filled statements.

Let's look a little deeper at what we are really saying when we say: "I can, and I will."

"Yes, I can!" implies that it is possible for me to do what I say I can do. It's a statement of faith that I "can" do this or that. But a critical question remains: "Will I?"

The ability to do something requires potential. The doing of it requires will. I may be capable of accomplishing something, and yet I'll never do it if I don't have the will to follow through with the planning and effort needed to see it to fruition.

There is a lot I can do that I may never do. Think about it. Who do you know who lives up to their full potential? I can always do more. I can always improve and do better. Notice how many times I just said, "I can"? The biggest question is: Will I?

To say "I can" is not a commitment. To say "I will" is a commitment.

Can you accomplish more? Can you achieve something better than you have ever achieved before?

Will you? That is a question only you can answer.

There is an old saying: *Can't never could and won't never will.*

Consider this . . . where in your life could you replace can't with can, and won't with will?

Prayer

Heavenly Father, please help me to believe I can when others, and even my own self-talk, says I can't. Then help me take action to do what I can for Your Kingdom.

Think/Act

Make a list of things you want to do. Consider how you can move some or all of those into the "I Did" list. Share your greatest victories with others.

_____

_____

_____

_____

The Common Denominator of Success: Wisdom from 1940

For if you live according to the flesh you will die; but if by the
Spirit you put to death the deeds of the body, you will live.
Romans 8:13

What I want to do (in my flesh) is not usually best. What I need to do is not always what I want to do at the time. Therefore, I have a dilemma. My guess is that you do, too! Have you ever not wanted to go to the gym for a workout you knew you needed to do? Have you ever wanted to eat something, but knew you didn't need to eat it? Have you ever wanted to say something harmful to someone who hurt you or made you mad, but knew you shouldn't say it? Have you ever wanted to skip reading the Bible for a period of time, or not take time to pray? I could go on. If you answered yes to any question above . . . read on.

When attendees arrived at the 1940 National Association of Life Underwriters annual convention in Philadelphia, they didn't realize they were about to witness one of the most profound presentations on success ever given. The address they were about to hear would not only impact them but would go down in history as a classic.

Albert Gray, an official for Prudential Life Insurance Company, delivered an address he called: "The Common Denominator of Success."

In that address, Mr. Gray famously said,

> The common denominator of success—the secret of success of every person who has ever been successful—lies in the fact that he or she formed the habit of doing things that failures don't like to do." When I read that statement for the first time, it raised a couple of questions for me. Why do some people like to do things that make them successful, and some don't like to do those things? Is that even fair? Are some people set up for success because they naturally like to do the things successful people do, while others just don't?

> I only had to read a couple of paragraphs further to find the answer. In anticipation of those very questions, Gray said: The things that failures don't like to do are the very things that you and I and other human beings, including successful men (and women), naturally don't like to do. In other words, we've got to realize right from the start that success is something which is achieved by the minority . . .

Note to reader: Albert Gray may have been considering Matthew 7:13–14 where we are told: "narrow is the gate and difficult is the way which leads to life, and there are few who find it."

So, do successful people actually like to do the things that you and I don't like to do? Gray says: "They don't!"

So, if they don't, then why do they do the things they don't like to do?

He said:

> *. . . the successful have a purpose strong enough to make them form the habit of doing things they don't like to do in order to accomplish the purpose they want to accomplish.*

Because you're reading this book titled *49 Days Back to ~~Normal~~ Better*, odds are good that you are interested in being one of those people who is successful.

If what Albert Gray said is correct, and I believe it is, then you must be very clear on the purpose that will pull you forward when the right action is unappealing.

What is the purpose that you want to accomplish more than anything else? What is it that you need to do—regardless of whether you WANT to do it—in order to accomplish that purpose?

You have a choice:

1. Do what you don't want to do (in the flesh) to get what you really want, or . . .
2. Only do what you want to do when you want to do it, and give up on what you truly desire deep inside.

Which will you choose?

Prayer

Heavenly Father, please help me to overcome my flesh and move past feelings so I can do what needs to be done, even though I don't feel like doing it.

Think/Act

Consider the two choices above. Which is best? Why? What will you do?

_____

_____

_____

_____

_____

_____

_____

_____

_____

_____

_____

Day 9

Two Things Everyone Has

As each one has received a gift, minister it to one another, as good stewards of the manifold grace of God. If anyone speaks, let him speak as the oracles of God. If anyone ministers, let him do it as with the ability which God supplies, that in all things God may be glorified through Jesus Christ, to whom belong the glory and the dominion forever and ever. Amen.

1 Peter 4:10–11

Delight yourself also in the Lord,
and He shall give you the desires of your heart.

Psalm 37:4

Consider this passage adapted from the book, *Every Day is Game Day* . . .

Desire and potential are precursors to the discovery and pursuit of purpose. No one has ever discovered his/her purpose or truly attempted to live according to that purpose without first having desire co-mingled with potential. In the following days, you will begin the process of discovering your purpose by understanding the power of the desire and potential that you already possess. The two things everyone, regardless of age, race, gender, IQ or nationality has in common is that they were born with desire and potential.

You have a ton of desires. That's easy to recognize. You think about those desires all the time. Some are good, fulfilling, and God directed. Some are not. While it's hard sometimes to sort it all out on your own, God has given us His Holy Spirit to help guide us along the way. Delight yourself in the Lord and your desires will line up with His will, and He will give you the desires of your heart. It always works out better that way. Always.

What's hard for some people to recognize is that you also have a ton of potential talent! By ton, we mean you have enough potential talent to accomplish with excellence the good works God Himself has prepared beforehand for you to do. You can't see it, but it's there.

World records will be broken every year. What was once seen as impossible is now seen as normal. Consider the Wright brothers trying to prove people can fly when many believed it would never happen. As of June 6, 2019, the Federal Aviation Administration estimated that 2,789,971 passengers fly in and out of US airports every day.

Prayer

Heavenly Father, help me fully understand that all things are possible with You. Sometimes I am held back by my limiting thoughts. I want to go back to better. Please help me see all things are possible through You. Help me understand what is possible.

Think/Act

What do you believe is impossible for you to accomplish? Are you doing everything you can with the ability God supplies? Is it possible that what you believe impossible could be possible?

_____

_____

_____

_____

_____

_____

_____

_____

_____

_____

_____

_____

_____

Day 10

The Dichotomy of Potential

Then God said, "Let the earth bring forth grass, the herb that yields seed And the fruit tree that yields fruit according to its kind, whose seed is in itself, on the earth"; and it was so.

Genesis 1:11

Imagine holding an apple seed in the palm of your right hand and a pebble in your left.

Now think about the potential of the apple seed you are holding. It is bountiful! That small seed holds within it the capacity to become a fruit bearing apple tree. This could be a beautiful tree that provides shade and produces delicious apples year after year. You might imagine the apples from that tree baked into a hot apple pie with ice cream on top.

Inside every apple this tree produces will be more apple seeds. So, you could potentially be holding an entire apple orchard in one hand. . . . all because of that one little seed. The number of apples which can be produced from that one little seed is unlimited. Its potential is endless.

Now think about that pebble you are holding in your left hand. What is the potential of that one little pebble? Unlike the apple seed, the pebble only has the potential to be a pebble. It will never grow into a rock. It can never become a boulder, or someday aspire to be a mountain. It is what it is, and it is what it will always be. It is a pebble.

Herein lies the *Dichotomy of Potential*. God has given you more potential than you can imagine.

However, with all of the potential packed inside the apple seed, there is an equal amount of opportunity to disappoint. Without proper care, soil, water, and sunshine, the seed would rot away and never become an apple tree. All of that wonderful potential would be fruitless.

The pebble, on the other hand, will never let you down. It is already living up to its full potential. You are always safe from disappointment if you stick with the pebble.

But is that what you really want? I think not. That's just not the way God made us.

I believe we were created to thrive on hope, the promise of potential. Without hope, life has no promise. Without promise, hope has no life. You are more like the apple seed than the pebble. You have potential, even if you do not always aspire to reach it.

When you deny your potential, you are like an apple seed acting like a pebble.

Your potential belongs to you. It is God given, just like the talents in the parable. What you do with it is determined by you. You can't grow an orchard overnight, and you can't get results from a seed that is never planted. Act today, and the results will follow.

Prayer

Heavenly Father, please help me understand that in You I have unlimited potential. You can do great work through me. Then help me to take appropriate action. Nothing is impossible for You.

Think/Act

Buy a package of apple seeds. Hold one apple seed in one hand and a pebble in the other. Consider the difference in potential between the two. Write something about your own potential and how, like an apple seed, that potential is vast. Determine what action you will take next to experience fruition of your potential in various areas of your life. Commit and act.

_____

_____

_____

_____

_____

_____

_____

_____

_____

_____

Day 11
Beyond the Quick Fix

So, Sarai said to Abram, "See now, the Lord has
restrained me from bearing children. Please, go in to my
maid; perhaps I shall obtain children by her."
And Abram heeded the voice of Sarai.
Genesis 16:2

o you remember the catchy jingle about being stuck on Band Aid? If not, you can find it on the internet and listen to it. If you do, you just might be singing it all day now that you have thought about it again! It was written to advertise the Band Aid brand of adhesive bandages, and their marketing strategy has been very effective. How many people do you know who ask for a "Band Aid" when they need an adhesive bandage? Have you ever thought of Band Aid as only being one brand of adhesive bandages? That's all it is. It's just a brand, introduced in 1920, which is distributed by the American pharmaceutical and medical-devices company Johnson & Johnson.

The only problem with this jingle is that it also seems to be the theme song of many people when it comes to productivity. Too many people are stuck on the "Band Aid method" of problem solving. It appears to be a life philosophy for so many people. They just stick a "Band Aid" on everything and hope for the best.

This reminds me of a story of a man who placed a Band Aid over the "Check Engine" light on the dashboard of his car. It hid the annoying light, and he didn't have to worry about that engine again—until one night when his car stopped on a dark country road ten miles from the nearest house. The Band Aid masked the problem temporarily but didn't actually solve anything. Too many people are looking for a quick fix when the truth is that quick fixes in life are few and far between.

Are you a quick-fix, Band Aid problem solver? Or do you take a more practical approach?

The Band Aid approach certainly is attractive because it's so quick and easy. A quick fix may be very easy to justify, but it is not always as expedient as it seems. You may save yourself a few hours or a few dollars now, but the long-term cost could be exponentially higher.

Always consider broader, more extensive solutions before settling on the Band Aid.

Sometimes, a Band Aid really is all that is needed. A quick and simple fix may be the best fix. You wouldn't put a tourniquet on a paper cut. However, it's always best to circle back around later to make sure the Band Aid approach is still working.

Whether you choose the easy fix or the tougher long-term solution, it's important to follow through and follow up. Always assess the level of success or failure of your actions. Continue to learn from your successes and mistakes.

God promised Sarai and Abram a child, but at a point, they started looking for a quick fix. When a Band Aid solution is misapplied, the consequences can linger for a very long time . . . some consequences can linger into generations.

Don't be a quick fix junkie. Don't get stuck on Band Aid solutions!

Prayer

Heavenly Father, please help me see beyond the quick and easy fix. Please help me not to be stuck on the quick Band Aid approach to situations in life.

Think/Act

Consider one area in life where you have applied the quick fix/Band Aid approach. How did that work out for you in the short-term? . . . long-term? Where are you tempted to take that approach now? Consider what you can do beyond quick fixes and band aids. Focus on long-term solutions and benefits.

_____

_____

_____

_____

_____

_____

_____

_____

_____

_____

_____

_____

_____

_____

_____

_____

_____

_____

_____

_____

_____

_____

_____

_____

3 Things Common People Do

He who observes the wind will not sow, And he who regards the clouds will not reap.
Ecclesiastes 11:4

People who have uncommon influence on others are uncommon people. By definition, most people are common. Let's consider three things common people do first.

The first of the three things common people do is to **accept.** Common people accept where they are as where they were meant to be. They believe what they can see in their current situation; they just accept it and go on with life, sometimes walking in fear and doubt.

In 2 Kings, we read that the city where Elisha and his men were staying was surrounded by an army. Elisha's servant saw the army and was afraid. He believed what he could see is what he had to accept. That's common. However, Elisha was uncommon. He saw more.

*And Elisha prayed, "Open his eyes, Lord, so that
he may see." Then the Lord opened the servant's eyes,
and he looked and saw the hills full of horses
and chariots of fire all around Elisha.*
2 Kings 6:17, ESV

The second thing is that Common people **settle.** Once they accept the faulty belief that their situation will never change, they begin to settle. Nothing stirs within them because they believe there is no reason to try to change, no reason to try to alter their own current reality. They get a false sense of comfort in settling and that begins to outweigh the vision of something better.

The third thing common people do is **stop.** Once they accept their own current reality and become comfortable in the settlement, they stop. Why try? Why dream? Why do anything differently? So, they just stop like the farmer who will not sow or reap.

You were not created to be common! There is only one of you in the world. There will never again be anyone exactly like you. No one else has your DNA. No one else can be you. *You are here for a greater purpose than to just accept the way things are.* You are here to do more than settle. And you should never stop. There is more you can do. There are bigger dreams for you to dream and accomplish. There are other people who need you to be uncommon so you can have uncommon influence on them. They need to see that their lives can change by seeing yours change.

Prayer

Heavenly Father, please help me to not just accept, settle, and stop. Help me to press on toward the goal for the prize of the upward call of God in Christ Jesus.

Think/Act

Consider the following questions . . .

1. Where are you just accepting the way things are in life?

_____

_____

2. If you want to go back to better, shouldn't you expect better effort from yourself?

_____

_____

3. Where are you settling for something that isn't best?

_____

_____

4. Is second best good enough when you could/should strive for what is best?

_____

_____

5. In what areas have you stopped dreaming, planning, and doing what needs to be done that could produce even better results in your life?

_____

_____

6. Now, what will you do? By when?

_____

_____

_____

_____

_____

_____

_____

_____

_____

_____

_____

_____

Day 13

3 Things Uncommon People Do

*And let us not grow weary while doing good, for in due
season we shall reap if we do not lose heart.*
Galatians 6:9

Uncommon people question. They don't just accept the status quo or the way they have been told things should be. They're not afraid to ask the hard-hitting questions, beginning with their own motives and attitudes. Paul questioned why he did what he did. (Romans 7:15–20) Uncommon people don't just ask if they are good enough—they ask if they are the best they can be. They don't just ask if the results are good enough—they ask if the results are the best they can be.

Uncommon people stretch. They—and the results they achieve—become better, stronger, and faster because they reach out for more than what is commonly accepted by others. Paul pressed toward the mark. (Philippians 3:14). Uncommon people go beyond what's been done before and what's already been accomplished and create a new normal. Records are broken and new foundations are established. They go the extra mile.

But they don't stop there . . .

Uncommon people continue. They do not grow weary while doing good. They know in due season they will reap if they do not lose heart. (Galatians 6:9) Uncommon people continue to question and stretch. They push on further. Of course, there are times when they rest—and rest is good—but they never stop. To uncommon people, rest is an opportunity to recharge, reenergize, and get ready for more. Their vision always outdistances their current reality, which makes stopping not an option.

Prayer

Heavenly Father, thank you for giving me the ability to think and question certain things. Thank you for giving me the ability to stretch beyond where I am now and continue to move forward.

Think/Act

What is one thing in your life you should question? Here are some examples . . .

1. Where do I need to improve?

_____

_____

_____

2. How can I improve?

_____

_____

3. What do I need to learn?

_____

_____

4. Where do I need to stretch myself and press in?

_____

_____

5. In what areas are things going well where I need to continue?

_____

_____

_____

_____

_____

_____

_____

_____

_____

Day 14

Living a Transformed Life

*And do not be conformed to this world, but be transformed
by the renewing of your mind, that you may prove what is
that good and acceptable and perfect will of God.*
Romans 12:2

*D*o you remember working with Play-Doh as a kid? Remember what it felt like to squeeze the Play-Doh and compress (really mashing) it into some form? The Play-Doh conformed to your will whether you were shaping it into forms of people, animals, houses or whatever you wanted. That's what the world tries to do to us. It tries to squeeze and compress us into whatever shape it wants. Have you ever wondered why so many people's lives seem to be disfigured? It's because the pressures of this world have shaped them into something God didn't intend for them to be. If we are formed by the world's perspective (conform to it), we will look like, act like, and be like the world . . . and that is not a pretty picture.

We have all experienced times when *the worries of this life, the deceitfulness of wealth and the desires for other things come in and choke the word, making it unfruitful.* (see Mark 4:19) But that's not how God intended us to live. He designed us to live a transformed life, not conformed to this world but transformed by the renewing of our mind by His Holy Spirit so we *may prove what is that good and acceptable and perfect will of God.*

The way you think controls what you do, when you do it, and how it gets done. Everything begins with a thought. The way you think affects your attitude and how you respond to different situations. If you are always trying to copy someone else, then you're probably thinking that their behavior and their customs will get you what you ultimately want. The problem is that many people don't really know what they want. Many are chasing something other than what is *that good and acceptable and perfect will of God.* This is primarily because they have allowed themselves to be conformed to a world full of other people telling them what they should want. You see, it's an ugly and dangerous spiral. It's so easy to fall into that trap. If that's happened to you, you can change it.

If you are thinking the wrong thoughts, you will never be able to live the life you really want to live (the life that is centered on *that good and acceptable and perfect will of God).* There will always be something lacking. Your mind is where the invisible battles are fought. If you lose the invisible battles that are fought on the inside, you are in grave danger of losing the war that manifests itself on the outside. Today can be the day you are set free! Today can be the day you can help someone else be set free!

Prayer

Lord, thank You because I don't have to be conformed to (molded by) this world. Thank You for allowing me to be transformed by the renewing of my mind. Please help me to be renewed in my mind so I can be transformed.

Act/Think

Consider where in your life you may feel like Play Doh, always feeling squeezed, compressed, and formed into what the world says you should be. In what areas do you want to be transformed? In what areas do you need to be renewed in your mind? Where are you losing the invisible battles being fought in your mind? What can you do to change that? Where are you winning the invisible battles being fought in your mind? How can you win more?

_____

_____

_____

_____

_____

_____

_____

_____

_____

_____

Day 15

Plan to Win: Winners Have a Winning Game Plan

The plans of the diligent lead surely to plenty,
But those of everyone who is hasty, surely to poverty.
Proverbs 21:5

I n sports, individuals and teams have games on the schedule they call Game Day. They also have days scheduled for travel, practice, and rest. In life, Every Day is Game Day! Game Day is: "that day in which all of the past culminates with present actions to forever change the future." In the game we call "life," that day is *every day*. In order to have the life we want, we need to be consistently living at our peak. Each day counts.

And they have a Game Plan.

Every sports team has a plan for winning their next game. No matter who you are or where you are in your life or your career, you need a plan. What you do with that plan can make all the difference in winning or losing the game of life.

Planning is a vital part of the success equation in life and work.

There are many who are excited about the process of putting a vision and a plan together. They work hard to create beautiful plans that they are very passionate about. Still, they need to be reminded to go back and review them. They need accountability to stick with it.

To further complicate things, you may have more than one thing that you're keeping an eye on. You may have a plan for your personal life and one for your career. You may have plans for a non-profit organization you're passionate about, or a book you want to write. There is even power in putting together a game plan for your children/grandchildren. With so many different and important plans and projects, it can be difficult to juggle them all.

That's where a Playbook comes in handy.

In the past, many successful people would carry a three-ring binder which would hold their various plans for each area in their life. These binders would include a place for current project worksheets, notes, and travel itineraries. Today, there are apps which can be used to carry everything in your pocket or purse.

Successful people have a playbook because it helps them "keep everything in play"!

Prayer
Lord, please help me to have a winning game plan for life and help me to live according to that plan.

Think/Act
Do you have a game plan for life? If you do, are you living it? Is your plan working? If not, what do you need to do?

_____

_____

_____

_____

_____

_____

_____

_____

_____

_____

_____

_____

_____

_____

_____

_____

Day 16
Hurry Up and Be Patient

Whoever is patient has great understanding,
but one who is quick-tempered displays folly.
Proverbs 14:29

During busy holiday seasons we've all heard some crazy stories of people who weren't so patient, polite, or kind to others. This happened one year on the Friday after Thanksgiving, known to most people as "Black Friday," because it's the day many businesses get "in the black" for the year's profitability.

There were stories of fights in stores over gadgets, toys, and towels. Now, you might fully expect to hear about scuffles over TVs, but *towels*? At one local store, someone actually got a few teeth knocked out in a battle over a bit of terrycloth.

Imagine that in the season of giving!

Someone posted the following question on Facebook: "Why is it that, while driving, we want people behind us to be patient with us while we are not so patient with the people driving in front of us?"

Ian Percy, once said, "We judge others by their behavior. We judge ourselves by our intentions."

Think about it. If someone pulls out in front of you on a road and you feel the need to tap your breaks to slow down, what do you think about that person?

Have you ever pulled out onto a road in front of someone else causing them to feel the need to slam their breaks in order to prevent a collision? My guess is that you were more forgiving in your thoughts toward yourself than toward the person who caused you to feel the need to tap your breaks. At that point, we have judged the person in front of us by their behavior and judged ourselves by our intentions. We didn't mean to do it . . . we just didn't see the other vehicle. Even when we feel the need to hurry, it's best to mingle in a little patience.

Try a little patience. Smile more, be kinder, and slow down. You may be surprised at the responses you get . . . not only from others, but in your own peace of mind.

Prayer

Jesus, please help me to be patient where I need more patience. Help me to smile more, be kinder to others around me, and to slow down when I am going too fast.

Think/Act

Where do you need to have more patience? What causes you to be impatient? What do you believe is the root cause for impatience?

Smile a little bit more today. Watch the response in others. Do a random act of kindness and consider how people react.

_____

_____

_____

_____

_____

_____

_____

_____

_____

_____

_____

_____

_____

_____

_____

_____

_____

Day 17
Irrefutable Success on a Bad Day

*For our light and momentary troubles are achieving for us
an eternal glory that far outweighs them all.*
2 Corinthians 4:17 (NIV)

We've all experienced bad days. Some we've handled better than others.

In 1960, after serving two years in the Army, Elvis Presley accepted a role in the movie *G.I. Blues*. The soundtrack for that movie was a 1961 Grammy Nominee in the category of Best Soundtrack Album. The RCA G.I. Blues soundtrack went Platinum and was #1 for ten of the 111 weeks it was on the LP chart. One of the songs on that soundtrack describes a perfectly bad day. It's titled, "Didja'Ever" . . . it's about having a bad day. Have you ever had one?

I (Tim Hill) walked out on stage to deliver a sermon I believed God had given me for the 750 people who had gathered for a special service when I quickly realized there was a problem. The dry cleaners had mismatched my suit and I hadn't realized it until I was front and center under the lights. I had walked out on the stage wearing the jacket of one suit, and the pants of another. Of course, one lady behind me in the choir not only noticed it, she was about to pass out with laughter. What did I do? I preached the sermon!

> . . . *For the Lord does not see as man sees; for man looks at*
> *the outward appearance, but the Lord looks at the heart.*
> 1 Samuel 16:7

I (Tim Enochs) drove seventy miles to a Franklin Covey seminar on how to effectively use a planner/calendar. The problem was I made the trip the day before the seminar was scheduled to take place. Hey, I was early! What did I do? I drove back home told my peers what happened, then drove back the next day and learned how to use the planner/calendar. Then I got certified to teach the class myself!

Of course, that story may have brought new meaning to the following verse for me . . .

> *Come now, you who say,*
> *Today or tomorrow we will go to such a city . . ."*
> James 4:13a

I just got my today and tomorrows mixed up. Bad days happen to us all. No one is immune.

Prayer

Lord, please help me to understand that we all have bad days and that no one is immune to a bad day. Help me see bad days from Your perspective rather than mine.

Think/Act

Consider these two thoughts:

1. This won't last forever.

_____

_____

_____

_____

2. Good can come from a bad day.

_____

_____

_____

_____

_____

_____

_____

_____

Day 18
Self-Talk

. . . For out of the abundance of the heart
the mouth speaks.
Matthew 12:34 b

We've all done things we didn't want other people to know we were doing. For today's section on *Self Talk*, I (Tim Enochs) will share something I did that I didn't want other people to know I was doing. Romans 3:23 affirms that we have all sinned and come short of the glory of God. No one wants anyone in the world to know the wrong we've done, or in this case—are doing. There are also things that aren't wrong, but we still don't want other people to know. That was the case with me. I wasn't sinning; I was reading a book. It was the title of the book I didn't want anyone to see.

Imagine me taking a deep breath at this point before typing the next sentence. Ok, here goes . . . I was reading a book titled: *What to Say When You Talk to Your Self*, by Shad Helmstetter.

Alright, I said it.

While I was reading the book, I remember taking it to a restaurant during lunch when I thought I could get some reading done. It was a buffet. Don't laugh, I actually turned the book upside down on the table, making sure the cover/title was face down on the table so no one walking by could see what I was reading. I guess it just seemed strange to be reading a book to learn how to better talk to yourself. My issue was negative self-talk about the title.

The good news is that there are 1,151 reviewers on Amazon giving the book a solid 4 Star rating! So, I'm not the only one. The reality is that self-talk is important. What we say to others, as well as to ourselves, originates in our heart. If my heart is not right, what I say to others, as well as to myself, will not be right. According to *Psychology Today, this internal chatter can be cheerful and supportive or negative and self-defeating.*

> *Watch your words!*
> *There is power of life and death in the tongue.*
> Proverbs 18:21

Prayer

Heavenly Father, as David encouraged himself in the Lord (1 Samuel 30:6), help me to encourage myself and others.

Think/Act

What are you thinking about yourself in your heart? What words about yourself are coming out of your mouth? Keep track of this over a few days. Are there any trends? Is your self-talk positive or negative? Are you encouraging yourself in the Lord where needed, or are you condemning yourself in agreement with the world?

_____

_____

_____

_____

_____

_____

_____

_____

_____

_____

_____

_____

_____

_____

_____

_____

_____

_____

Day 19
Choose Wisely . . . Then Act

For as the body without the spirit is dead,
so faith without works is dead also.
James 2:26

Truett Cathy, Founder of Chick-fil-A, once shared a riddle about 5 birds sitting on a tree limb. He shared that 4 decided to fly off.

Truett then asked: How many are left?

The math is easy. 5 birds were there, subtract the 4 birds which decided to fly off, and the answer is easy . . . 1 bird left sitting on the tree limb.

The answer, however, is not that simple. You see, 4 birds "decided" to fly off. The riddle didn't state they actually did.

In life, there are many times we all get stuck in the decision process and never take action. There are also times when we actually make a decision and still not take action. What happens? Nothing.

Choose wisely . . . then . . . take action.

Prayer

Jesus, please give me the wisdom to make wise choices and then to take appropriate action. I understand that faith without works is dead.

Think/Act

Are you making wise choices? Then, are you acting on those choices?

Make a list of wise choices you've made and acted on over the past few weeks. How did it feel?

_____

_____

_____

_____

_____

_____

_____

_____

_____

_____

_____

What happens if you don't make wise choices or act on those wise choices?

_____

_____

_____

_____

_____

_____

_____

_____

_____

_____

_____

_____

_____

_____

_____

_____

_____

Day 20

A Time to Live

. . . whereas you do not know what will happen
tomorrow. For what is your life?
It is even a vapor that appears for a little time
and then vanishes away.
James 4:14

Note: Day 20 is dedicated to the families of Curtis Hill and the twenty-one others who lost their lives in the terrible accident that happened on October 29th, 1960.

Within the rich history of college football there is a story of tragedy, compassion, and second chances. The year was 1960, and the Cal Poly football team had just suffered a devastating 50–6 loss to Bowling Green University.

Hours after the game was over, members of the team boarded a bus in Toledo for the short ride to the airport where they were to catch their midnight flight back to San Luis Obispo. The fog that night was so dense that taxi service in the city was shut down. At the airport, the team made their way onto the tarmac toward the waiting plane. Through the fog, they could barely see the plane only a few short yards ahead.

As they boarded, wide receiver Curtis Hill asked senior quarterback Ted Tollner to change seats with him. Curtis had become ill that morning on the bumpy outbound flight and was hoping that a seat closer to the front of the plane would make for a smoother ride home. Ted agreed and moved several rows back to Curtis' original seat. Soon, the plane was rolling down the runway and the team settled in for the long flight home.

But then, just as the plane began making the climb to cruising altitude, tragedy struck.

The left engine gave out, and the plane slammed into the ground, splitting into two pieces. Twenty-two people lost their lives in the crash. Twenty-six survived.

In the weeks following this tragedy, the compassion and outpouring of emotional support for the survivors and the families of those who perished was truly amazing. However, it is the impact of a second chance at life that amazes me most.

Curtis Hill, who had requested to change seats with Ted Tollner, lost his life in the crash. Ted survived. The row in which Ted was seated was the first row of survivors. In Ted's words: "I was the cutoff for who lived and died, everyone in front of me died . . . everyone behind me survived. How do you explain this? There is no explanation."

It was not Ted's time to leave this world. He had more to accomplish, and he never forgot that.

Ted went on to have a career as a coach and continues to make a difference in the lives of a multitude of people on and off the field. Quarterback Steve Young gave credit to Ted during his

Hall of Fame speech. Ted's influence also extends through the lives of his children. His son, Bruce, co-wrote a book entitled *The C.H.I.L.D. Game Plan*, which was inspired by many of the lessons he learned from his father.

When you consider the effect of Ted's life—the players he has coached, the friends he has helped, the children he has raised—it adds up to a life of significance. And he isn't finished yet! Ted realized the value of the extra time he was given, and he is making the most of it.

Prayer

Heavenly Father, as we are instructed in Psalm 90:12, help me to realize that my days are numbered and that I only have a brief time in this life to do what you have called me to do. Please help me to understand that urgency and act in it each day that I am alive.

Think/Act

Since you are reading this book, then you haven't yet arrived at "your time to go." None of us know when that time will be. The real question is, *what will you do with the time you have left?* Stop practicing at life—the clock is already running!

_____

_____

_____

_____

_____

_____

_____

_____

_____

_____

_____

_____

_____

_____

_____

_____

_____

_____

_____

_____

_____

_____

Day 21
What's Growing in Your Backyard?

*You shall not sow your vineyard with different kinds of
seed, lest the yield of the seed which you have sown and
the fruit of your vineyard be defiled.*
Deuteronomy 22:9

*M*ost every speaker has had the opportunity to hear good reports as a result of connecting with individuals through a sermon, keynote presentation, speaking at executive and team retreats, etc. One of the most rewarding experiences for a speaker is when someone reports of a speech, sermon, or presentation being life-changing for an attendee. Although it is always very pleasing to hear, most speakers realize that it wasn't all about them as a speaker. They understand they only scattered some seeds. In most cases, it was someone else who prepared the soil and tended to the seeds once they were planted. The combination of these conditions can produce much fruit.

The same principle is true for every aspect of life. It's really that simple. Some of the most important questions any of us can ask ourselves include . . .

1. How are you preparing the soil for the seed?
2. What seeds are you scattering?
3. How are you tending seeds which have already been planted?

During the decade of the 1950s, Earl Nightingale recorded *The Strangest Secret*. During that recording, he states: *The soil doesn't care what you plant. The fertile soil of the mind will grow whatever seeds you plant, not caring if what you plant is good or bad.*

Whatever is planted will grow.

If you have weeds growing in your life or business, it's because that is what you or someone else planted. If you have a great harvest of fruit, then you have planted the right seeds.

If you want to know what seeds you've planted in your lawn of life, ask yourself . . .

What's growing in my backyard?

Once you fully understand and apply this principle, you will be well on your way!

Prayer

Lord, I need help to choose which seeds to plant in the lawn of my life. Please help me to always choose good seeds, not weeds.

Think/Act

Consider, what's growing in the backyard of your life? What's growing in the back will always find its way to the front. Where in your life (front yard or back) do you need to pull weeds and plant different seeds? What do you want to grow there? What are you planting and watering?

Day 22
Jet Envy

But earnestly desire the best gifts.
And yet I show you a more excellent way.
1 Cor 12:31

Everyone wants to be successful. But what does that mean? How do you know when you have achieved true success?

I'll never forget a trip I (Tim Enochs) took several years ago to interview some potential engineers for our organization. We flew in a private plane, which was a major improvement over driving. It felt good to arrive in the morning and complete the interviews, knowing I would be back at home that afternoon.

There was a plane taking off ahead of us: a private jet. They only needed half the runway to take off; in our prop *puddle-jumper*, we needed every foot of it. The people ahead of us would be flying higher and faster! I remember thinking how much better it would be if we only had a jet.

Not long afterwards, I moved to a different company. We had a jet. I felt I had arrived.

That is, until one day we were in Florida getting ready to fly home. We were delayed due to a thunderstorm and had to wait it out at the airport. It was a small airport and there were several other private jet owners and pilots waiting out the storm. I overheard our pilot speaking with another pilot about how nice that pilot's jet was compared to ours.

It wasn't long before I was looking at other jets wishing our jet were bigger and faster, with even more luxurious leather seats. That's when I heard an elderly lady asking her pilot which jet they would be taking that day. He replied, "Well, it's such a short trip, I thought we would take the small jet." I finally realized there was no end in sight.

First, I realized it was better to fly than to drive. Then, I wanted a jet rather than a prop plane. On my first trip in our private jet, I wished for a nicer jet. Then I was somewhat appetent to hear that someone had a choice between two jets. Would three jets be enough?

Every time I got what I wanted it quickly became not good enough. My definition of success was refutable. It was based on comparison and possession. It was all centered around me.

Irrefutable Success is different. It is defined as being in a continual state of doing the absolute best I can, with what I have, in order to have a positive influence on other people. That is the kind of success that pays huge dividends in your life and mine.

We all have positive and negative influences on each other, whether we know it or not. It's only when we are intentional about having a positive influence that we shift the pendulum away from the negative. The outcome is nothing short of miraculous.

Today, I measure success by the quality of impact I have on those around me, and not by the quality of leather seats on a private jet.

Prayer

Heavenly Father, please help me measure success only by the quality of impact I have on those around me. Having nice *things* is fine, as long as they don't define or consume me. Success is not in things. The quality of impact I have on those around me can last forever and can be used by You to make their lives and mine better. Please help me desire a more excellent way.

Think/Act

How do you measure success? Is there a more excellent way? Please encourage others by sharing your more excellent way of measuring success.

_____

_____

_____

_____

_____

_____

_____

Check Your Own Shoe First

So, David's anger was greatly aroused against the man . . .
2 Samuel 12:5

Then Nathan said to David, You are the man!
2 Samuel 12:7

*J*im Rohn once said, "If you want something to change, change yourself."

Recently, a friend of mine was meeting with a group of people when he detected the distinct smell of something someone's pet had left on the lawn. He looked around the room, trying to discern who could have tracked in this unpleasant odor, but saw no obvious signs of guilt or even awareness on the face of anyone else in the room.

Without a known culprit, there was nobody with whom he could address the situation. How could someone just stand there and not realize they had stepped in something with such a foul smell?

After completing his meeting in the room, he was more than happy to escape the smell. But as he got into the car and began to drive away, he realized with a sense of dread that he could still smell the foul odor, only now it was even stronger.

Then it hit him . . . he was the guilty one.

He confirmed the grisly truth. He was the culprit. He was the one responsible for bringing that smell into the meeting room. How could it be that, while searching for the offender, he was the guilty one all along?

But that's just how it is with many things in our lives. While looking for faults in others, we fail to see our own. We blame our situation on people or circumstances, and we overlook our own culpability. We need to look at ourselves first.

Here's a great question to consider, "Why do you look at the speck of sawdust in your brother's eye and pay no attention to the plank in your own eye?" (Matthew 7:3) In other words, how can you judge others—or even help them improve—when you are ignoring your own faults and limitations?

When you take the time to "check your own shoe" first, you will be in a much better position to have a positive impact on others!

Prayer

Jesus, please help me to always consider where I may need to change rather than assuming others need to change first.

Think/Act

Make it a practice to always consider your own ways before correcting others. While that could keep most of us busy for a while, it's always the best discipline. You might be surprised what you find on the bottom of your shoe.

Day 24
Nothing But the Truth

Kings take pleasure in honest lips;
they value the one who speaks what is right.
Proverbs 16:13 (NIV)

*A*s King of Israel, Solomon was best known for his wisdom and his wealth. Drawing from Solomon's teachings, Pat Williams, former Senior Vice President of the Orlando Magic wrote, *Leading With Integrity, The 28 Essential Leadership Strategies of Solomon.*

Pat knows a little something about leadership wisdom. In his former position as the Senior Vice President for the Orlando Magic, he has played an integral role in the birth of the team and its success. He is a best-selling author of more than sixty-five books and is a sought-after speaker who inspires people around the world.

Here's one of the strategies from the chapter entitled "Truth, Inc."

People need to know the "unedited and undistorted truth." A person can have all of the leadership skills in the world, but without truth, the skills will be ineffective. A successful person must be armed with unfiltered, reliable information if they are to make informed choices.

People who become isolated or insulated from accurate and timely information can become anemic and insipid. No one needs "yes-men" who try to make them happy by ignoring the elephant in the room. As Pat puts it: "The 'elephant' is any issue that is so big and scary that people (though aware of it) are afraid to speak about it openly." What people need is candor and open lines of communication. People need to know about the elephant.

Speak the truth and appreciate when others to do the same.

Solomon says, "Good leaders cultivate honest speech; they love advisors who tell them the truth" (Proverbs 16:13).

Prayer

Jesus, I know the truth can set me and others free. Please help me to always focus on truth no matter whether it is easy or hard to accept.

Think/Act

Are there any areas where you may struggle with truth?

_____

_____

_____

_____

_____

What should you do?

_____

_____

_____

_____

_____

_____

_____

How can you make truth the focal point of everything you think, say, and do?

_____

_____

_____

_____

_____

_____

_____

_____

_____

Set Free by the Power of Truth

And you shall know the truth, and the truth shall make
you free.
John 8:32

The enemy wants you to be bound. God wants you free. The ultimate choice is yours. Do you want to be free?

Consider this story from *The Street Sweeper.* A young man had a decision to make. He could lie and go free or tell the truth and get a speeding ticket.

> How can the truth set you free when it seems that a little white lie can reduce trouble in your life? Let me share something that happened to me when I was in college. One night, I was put in a very challenging situation. While driving a female friend home, I was stopped by a police officer for speeding. The officer asked me to step out of the car. I couldn't help but wonder why he wanted me to step out of the car. I had never been asked to step out of a car because

of speeding before; however, I obviously needed to comply with the officer's request.

I thought, perchance, if the officer were having a good night, he might let me off with a warning. What followed was a dialogue that still perplexes me today:

"Do you realize you were speeding?"

"Yes sir, I do."

"Do you understand that I could write a ticket that would cost you or your parents $110?"

"Yes sir, I do."

"Were you wearing your seatbelt?"

"Yes sir, I was." (I always wore a seat belt.)

"Well, I didn't see you wearing your seat belt. If you will tell me that you were not wearing it, I'll give you a warning for speeding and fine you for not wearing a seatbelt. That ticket will cost you $10, which you can probably pay, and your parents will never find out about it."

I replied, "Sir, I can't lie to you; I was wearing a seat belt."

"OK, if that's the way it is, I am writing the higher citation for speeding." He wrote the speeding ticket and handed it to me.

Startled by the exchange of conversation, I got back into the car and drove away. The next day I called my dad and explained what happened.

How do you think he responded? He had two very different responses to the situation:

First . . .

"Son, you know you should not have been breaking the speed limit. We have discussed this before, and you know the law."

"Yes sir, I do."

Then . . .

"Now that we have cleared that up, based on the circumstances after you were stopped for speeding, I am so proud of you and am thrilled that you took the option to accept the speeding ticket rather than lie. Thank you for being honest. This is one ticket I will be happy to pay for you."

After hearing this story, some people may think I was pretty slick in creating an amazing story like that to ease my dad's response to my getting a ticket. The fact is that I had always been honest with my dad and he trusted me to always tell the truth. I was free to tell my dad an otherwise unbelievable true story because our relationship was built on a foundation of truth. Did we have to pay the ticket? Yes. Well, my dad paid it. Was I free inside because I told the truth? Absolutely. The truth will always set you free—even if it seems to cost you in the short run.

—Excerpt from: *The Street Sweeper*.

Prayer

Heavenly Father, I know there are no *little lies*, please help me to always understand and operate in truth.

Think/Act

Is there any area in your life where you may not be accepting or acting on absolute truth? While you are hopefully not spreading lies, is there any area where you may be believing a lie?

Note: Craig Groeschel's book Winning The War In Your Mind *is a great resource. Chapter 1, "Perception Is Reality," is powerful and is a great place to start.*

Day 26

The Pain of Pre-Season

*Do you not know that those who run in a race
all run, but one receives the prize?
Run in such a way that you may obtain it.*
1 Corinthians 9:24

There is something about a crisp evening in early fall that brings a sense of anticipation in the heart of every football fan. Friday night lights on a high school football field marked with white lines and hash marks chase the growing darkness away. Smoke from the concession stand drifts out over the field, carrying the char-grilled aroma of hamburgers and hot dogs, while the marching band strikes up the local school fight song right after playing the national anthem . . . for a brief moment, everything seems right in the world.

This could be our year!

Every new season holds promise. Every team starts with the same record. Everybody is tied for first place. All of the practice in the hot August sun could pay dividends of games won and championships to be remembered forever. Time seems to stand still . . . and then the whistle blows and the ball is kicked high into the air. The game is on!

A true football fan loves the game for what it is—some prefer high school, some college and some pro football. For others, the only thing that matters is that it's football.

Every game matters. In the NFL, the first few pre-season games are a chance for coaches to observe their team in action against an actual opponent without it counting toward the ultimate outcome of the season. It's different than just practicing against your own team every day. While this is good for the teams to get ready for "the real thing," it can be difficult for fans.

One person posted on Facebook, "Why is pre-season football so painful to watch?"

During pre-season, for the most part, it's not the starters playing most of the game. Even hard-fought victories don't count toward the record. From all appearances, the outcome doesn't matter. But something does matter during pre-season. It matters a lot! The new guys are working hard to make the team. Their future is on the line. The future chemistry of the team is on the line. It does all count for something; it's just harder to see.

Casual fans are all about the thrill of the championship game, when the stakes are high, and the superstars are playing at their peak. Some people only watch the playoffs, some only the Super Bowl, and there are some who only watch the commercials during the Super Bowl. But students of the game realize that no team ever won a championship by coasting during the pre-season and practices. Success begins by playing hard and making it count, even if no one is keeping score.

Prayer

Lord, help me to see the value and take full advantage of every minute, even those that don't seem to matter.

Think/Act

What you do as soon as you wake up in the morning and just before you retire for the evening can make a huge difference in your life. Consider that time your "*Pre*-Season" for a championship day. Your morning routine and your evening routine are critical to set the stage for a productive day and much needed rest at night.

Make a list of what you believe you should be doing each morning and each evening. Then, for a week, track what you actually do. Are you consistently doing what you should be doing? Do you have established disciplines of a champion in place? This is your time, when no one else is looking, and no one is keeping score. Play it like a champion. You just might be surprised with the results.

_____

_____

_____

_____

_____

_____

_____

_____

Day 27

Life Can Be Unfair . . . So?

For the Lord God will help Me;
Therefore I will not be disgraced;
Therefore I have set my face like a flint,
And I know that I will not be ashamed.
Isaiah 50:7

In my book, *Furnace Grace*, I (Tim Hill) wrote:

Trouble has a way of finding all of us. Like the rain, it comes to the just and the unjust. We would like to believe that Christians are exempt from trouble, but not so. Job expressed it rather somberly in Job 14:1: "Man who is born of woman is of few days and full of trouble."

Trouble may come in the form of a single catastrophe, or it may come in a multiplicity of small things like a plague of grasshoppers. It may come from a most surprising source or from an ongoing problem. Sometimes it comes from our own folly and sin, but often it is not directly traceable to us at all.

Trouble can announce itself with a telephone call in the wee hours of the morning or by a visit to a somber-faced doctor. Yes, trouble can come in the form of a serious diagnosis and a worse prognosis from a doctor. It can be caused by the impact of colliding cars, a note in your pay envelope, or the gradual erosion of a debilitating disease. It seems that trouble is the rule, rather than the exception, and none can prevent it from happening. Although we cannot control trouble, we can control our reaction when it comes our way. We have the ability to determine whether it will make us sweet or bitter.

Etched in the annals of antiquity is a story about a boy named Joseph who had vivid dreams about becoming a leader. The first time he had this dream, he only shared it with his brothers. The second time, he also told his father about it. His father rebuked him, and then wondered what the dream meant. His brothers, who were already jealous, hated him.

One day Joseph's father sent him on a journey to check on his brothers who were working away from home. When they saw him approaching, they said "Here comes the dreamer, let's kill him and tell our father he was killed by a wild animal." Joseph's brother, Reuben, wanting to save Joseph's life, convinced them to throw him into a pit instead.

While Joseph was in the pit, the other brothers seized an opportunity to sell him to some passing slave traders. The slave traders travelled to a nearby country and sold Joseph to a man who was captain of the King's royal guard.

Joseph served diligently and was soon promoted to the position of Assistant to the Captain. Eventually, he was given complete administrative responsibility for everything the captain owned. Things seemed to be going well until the day Joseph was wrongly accused of attempting to seduce the Captain's wife. Upon hearing the news, the Captain threw Joseph into the prison.

Joseph quickly found favor with the prison warden and was placed in charge of all of the prisoners. During this time, Joseph shared his dream interpreting wisdom with two prominent prisoners. True to Joseph's interpretation, one was released and restored to his position as Cup Bearer to the King. The released prisoner had promised to help Joseph, but after his release he forgot all about his promise.

Finally, after two years when the King needed help interpreting a dream, the Cup Bearer remembered Joseph. He was summoned from the prison, shared his wisdom with the King, and was immediately released. Joseph used his God-given wisdom and insight to prepare the nation during seven years of good harvest followed by seven years of drought and famine. His plan worked so well that, along with providing for that nation, there was enough to help nearby nations.

By this time, Joseph was second-in-command of the entire nation. Joseph's initial dreams of leadership had come to fruition, and when his brothers (who didn't even recognize him) arrived asking him for help, he was able to provide for them too.

There are at least three principles we can learn from this story of Joseph:

1. **Joseph never allowed any person or circumstance, no matter how unfair, to cause him to waver in what he knew he should do.** Of course, it is always good to seek wise counsel. The problem is there can be jealous people who only want to hold you back, or who only see things through the filter of their own best interests. There are also people who simply don't share your dream or vision. Don't allow them to get you off course.

2. **Regardless of circumstance or position, Joseph did excellent work with the gifts he had been given.** You can't control everything that happens, but you can control yourself. Wherever you are, do your best. You never know who is watching, and even if no one is paying attention, you will know inside your own heart whether or not you are giving your best effort. Excellent work is always worthwhile, whether in prison or in the throne room.

3. **Joseph had compassion on those who treated him unfairly.** Most people have all been treated unfairly, an react to that unfair treatment differently. If you think about the times you were vindictive, compared to the times you fought through the urge to strike back, you will most likely see that taking the high road is the path that usually leads to a quicker and stronger resolution.

Prayer

Lord, please help me to set my face like a flint. Help me to never allow any person or circumstance, no matter how unfair, to waver in doing what I know I should do. Please help me, regardless of circumstance or position, to always do excellent work with the gifts You have given me. Help me to always have compassion, even on those who treat me unfairly.

Think/Act

Consider the following questions:

1. What could cause you to waver in doing what you know you should do? How can you prevent that from happening?

_____

_____

_____

_____

_____

2. Are you doing excellent work with all of the gifts God has given you?

_____

_____

_____

_____

_____

_____

3. Do you have compassion on everyone? Even those who treat you unfairly?

_____

_____

_____

_____

_____

_____

_____

_____

_____

_____

_____

_____

_____

_____

_____

_____

_____

Day 28

Unimpressed with Elvis

But as for you, be strong and do not give up,
for your work will be rewarded.
2 Chronicles 15:7

S am Phillips opened the door to Memphis Recording
Service (now known as Sun Studio) on January 3,
1950. The following year, it earned the title of the
"Birthplace of Rock and Roll" when Jackie Brenston and Ike
Turner recorded the song *Rocket 88.*

Sam broke all the rules in the music business—not because
he was a rebel, but because he just didn't know the rules.

According to the Sun Studio website . . .

> He didn't know not to use much echo . . . a three-
> piece band sounded like an all-night party! He didn't
> know not to crank the amp up so high that it dis-
> torted. He didn't know not to blend the musical
> styles—or that it wasn't supposed to be sheer passion
> and fun. Rock N' Roll was created—with all these
> wonderful mistakes.

Once things really got to rocking, several musicians and singers in the Memphis area wanted to be part of what was going on at 706 Union Ave in Memphis, Tennessee. One of those hopeful musicians was a shy eighteen-year-old named Elvis Presley.

In July of 1953, Elvis walked into the studio with a dime-store guitar and a desire to record two songs titled: "My Happiness" and "That's When Your Heartaches Begin" for his mother.

This is where the story has an interesting twist. Many people assume Elvis walked in, sang a few bars, knocked the socks off the people at the studio, and walked out the King of Rock N' Roll.

The truth is, while Sam Phillips could see some raw potential in Elvis, he just wasn't sure what to do with him. As the story goes, Elvis hung around the studio for almost a full year before he was given another opportunity. Marion Keisker, who worked with Sam Phillips as his assistant, remembered that shy eighteen-year-old with raw talent and convinced Sam to give Elvis another shot.

Sam brought him back to record a couple of songs. But again, he was just not that impressed.

Then, weeks later Elvis was in the studio again and started playing *That's All Right (Mama)*. Something caught Sam's attention, and he began to record the track. Within three days it became a hit on Memphis radio and would soon spread across the nation. The rest is Rock 'N Roll history.

It would have been easy for Elvis to give up on his dreams in the face of adversity, but he persisted. Don't quit. Don't let one person's opinion stifle your dream. Stick around and keep on singing your song of life the way God created you to sing it. Only God knows what could happen. The rest is just noise.

Prayer

Jesus, stand with me whenever I feel like quitting. Please don't let me quit following Your calling on my life just because of what others might say.

Think/Act

Consider a time in life when you quit but should have continued. Why did you quit? Do you wish you hadn't quit? Now, consider a time when you fought through the urge to quit and kept going. Are you glad you didn't quit? While there may be a time to quit, be sure it's truly time to quit before you quit. Fight the urge to quit and Press On!

_____

_____

_____

_____

_____

_____

_____

_____

_____

_____

Day 29
A Question of Achievement

I press toward the goal for the prize of the upward call of
God in Christ Jesus.
Philippians 3:14

The following question was posted on Facebook:

What holds you back from achieving your goals?

There was no real surprise in the initial responses. However, there were lessons to be learned as we consider what keeps us from achieving the things we really want in life. Following are actual responses:

Response 1: "Other people's negative energy . . . I try to not let it get to me, but sometimes certain people have powerful effects on one's life and choices."

The people who surround us can have as much of an impact on our lives as we allow them to have—for better or for worse. Often, it's the people closest to us that hurt us the most. If someone close to you is holding you back from achieving your goals, it could be that they are jealous of what you are about to achieve. Achieve it anyway. Consider having a conversation with them to let them know that their negative energy is pulling you down. Express how important they are in your life, and that you need them to lift you up, not tear you down.

Response 2: My own excuses. I can't blame anyone for what I fail to prioritize . . .

This one probably hits home for most of us. Often, I can't truly lay the blame on anyone but myself. The key to fighting your own lack of priorities is to have a deep understanding of WHY you want what you want. This begins with a clear Vision and a Life Plan. When the understanding of "why" is strong, the motivation to achieve is great.

Response 3: Personal, and then again, myself.

This one was intriguing because this person has battled a physical illness that, at times, makes everything in life a challenge. We all struggle with forces beyond our control—physical limitations, environment, the economy, the weather, etc. The reality is that we still must look at ourselves and how we respond to outside forces. Often, what challenges us mostly can be used by God to pave the avenue to success.

Response 4: *The world.*

This one wins the prize for the biggest reason described in the fewest words! We have all experienced the weight of the world at some point in our lives. Everyday life can distract us from the destiny of greatness God has intended for the work He has given us to do. Every second of every minute of every hour of every day we are bombarded with something. We have all seen a lot of bumper stickers with some variation of this statement . . . but the truth is *Life Happens!*

It is important that we set our sight toward the direction of the goals God has placed in our heart. You may have heard it said that, *It's not the direction of the wind, but the set of your sails, that determine your course.* Let's be victors, not victims. We must be the ones to make right decisions and take charge of our own actions and reactions, then sail on. That is our God given, God ordained opportunity!

People who are going back to better face the same problems as everyone else. They achieve because they overcome problems and obstacles and press on *toward the goal for the prize of the upward call of God in Christ Jesus.*

Prayer

Heavenly Father, please help me to not let anything deter me from dreams and goals you have placed in my heart.

Think/Act

Make a list of every goal you can think of that you want to achieve. Pray about each and ask God to give you the appropriate desire for each goal. If you are honest with God and yourself, He will lead you and help keep the dreams and goals He wants you to achieve. You can walk away from the rest. Then go for it . . . go for all of it . . . press on toward whatever is still on your list and don't let anything or anybody get in your way.

_____

_____

_____

_____

_____

_____

_____

_____

_____

_____

_____

_____

_____

_____

_____

Day 30

There's Power in Asking

Ask, and it will be given to you . . .
Matthew 7:7

Following is an excerpt from the ebook: *7 Revelations for Irrefutable Success*:

The third revelation is something that many people believe they are really good at doing. It has to do with asking; but it's much deeper than that.

Just ask. Sounds simple enough, doesn't it?

You will receive every time you ask. You just may not receive what you expect.

When you ask, you will always receive one of three responses:

1. Yes (which means you get what you want right then),
2. Not now (there is a better time for you to receive), or
3. No (because there could be something even better that you will receive later). Sometimes, the timing is not right, and sometimes the motive of your request is not best. Sometimes, the full understanding will come after we get to Heaven.

Although the second and third responses may not seem good to you at the moment, your faith has to be strong in believing that God knows what is best. You must trust God throughout the process.

It is important to realize that you are asking for a reason. Sometimes that reason is to fulfill a need, while at other times, it is to fulfill a desire. It's the reason for which you are asking that is far more important than what you believe you want or need and when you believe you want or need it. The fact is that you are really asking for the fulfillment of something that is missing, whether it is something that fulfills a need or a desire. This is a very important concept for you to understand.

Does that mean that you should never ask for something specific? No, a thousand times no. In fact, it is important to be very specific when you ask. One day a man was working on landscaping his lawn. He asked his son to bring him a tie. Confused about why his dad wanted a tie, the bewildered boy went into the house and picked up one of his dad's neckties and brought it to him. The astonished man looked at his son and asked, 'Why did you bring this to me?' The son replied, 'You asked for a tie.' Looking at the boy, the man said, 'I wanted a railroad tie'—and they both laughed.

There are four rules for asking:

1. It is very important to know exactly what you are asking for. You can only do this after you have been honest with yourself and completely understand the reason you are asking. Only then are you prepared to ask for something specific.

2. Then you have to know who to ask. Who has the power to fulfill your request? A good rule to remember is to never accept no as an answer from someone who does not have the authority to say yes.

3. Now it is important to know when to ask. We are all guilty of asking the right question of the right person at the wrong time. When it comes to asking, timing is as important as location is to selling real estate.

4. It is also important to know how to ask. You can ask the same thing of multiple people and get very different responses because of how the question was asked. Are you asking in faith, or is doubt present at the door? If you aren't going to ask and believe, don't ask.

The final thing to remember when asking is that sometimes you have to keep asking. Sometimes you just have to be persistent.

Prayer

Lord, help me to keep asking. If needed, change my heart so I am asking for the right things, but please help me to keep asking until I fully understand Your answer.

Think/Act

Make a list of everything you are asking for and ask every day, maybe multiple times during a day. Ask Him to help you understand when He answers with the final answer . . . until then, keep asking.

_____

_____

_____

_____

_____

_____

_____

_____

_____

_____

_____

_____

_____

_____

_____

_____

_____

_____

The Value of Support

If the whole body were an eye,
where would be the hearing?
If the whole were hearing,
where would be the smelling?
But now God has set the members,
each one of them, in the body just as He pleased.
1 Corinthians 12:17–18

There is no way to accurately assess the value of support others have provided in your life. However, the support they have provided you along the way has a ripple effect on everyone you impact. There is a cascading effect which connects your life with everyone else involved. That's just the way God made it.

We all have different talents and callings on our life. One person's God-given talent is no greater than another person's God-given talent. The fact is, some people's gifts and callings are more visible than those of others, but they are no more important.

Take this book for example. The names on the cover are Tim Hill, Tim Enochs, and Adam Enochs. We are listed as authors. You are reading our words that we believe were thoughts inspired by God for us to write. But if all you had were our words, you might find typos, and all sorts of errors throughout the book. Our focus has been on content. Of course, we did our best to convey the thoughts God placed in our hearts, but He didn't set the process up for us to do it all. He gifted others to do their part, and they do their part much better than we could do their part.

There are editors, a publisher (which is actually a team of people), people in cover design, printing, sales, packaging and shipping. All of these people are working behind the scenes to provide the best reading experience they can for your enjoyment and profit. For example, one of the editors of this book has edited multiple books including a *New York Times* best-seller, and a book which was made into a movie which casted two Grammy winners and launched the careers of others. You don't know her name. Had she not completed her role with excellence, the *New York Times* best-seller may have never made it to print, much less hit the *New York Times* list. The owner of the film company may not have enjoyed the book enough to want to invest a large sum of money to make a movie based on the book. Had that not happened, one of the actors' career may have never been launched, Larry Gatlin would have never written the song he wrote for the movie, and *Through The Fire* by Jason Crabb may have never been seen on the big screen at the premiere in Nashville. An untold number of peoples' lives may have never been touched when they watched the movie on TBN.

Here's one more example. The person who painted the picture for the cover of the book that was made into a movie did a phenomenal job. It was a work of art! (pun intended) Had the cover of the book not been appealing, the filmmaker may have not been interested enough to open the book. Yet, you don't know that artist's name. Your knowing his name or the editor's name is not what is important to them. Doing excellent work in the good works God prepared in advance for them to do is what is more important to them.

You see where this is going? There are so many people involved in every aspect of our lives. Just because we can't see them doesn't mean they aren't there. They are.

Some people may never have their name in lights, but their work is there for all the world to see. They do excellent work to glorify their Father in heaven.

Let your light so shine before men,
that they may see your good works
and glorify your Father in Heaven.
Matthew 5:16

Prayer

Lord, please help me to always know that the good works You have given me to do are to glorify You, not me. They will be beneficial to others, and that benefits me. When my world is in Your order, everyone wins.

Think/Act

Consider the following questions.

1. How have you let your light shine in the past so that others have seen your good works?

_____

_____

_____

_____

_____

_____

2. Is there anything that you should be doing that you haven't started? When will you start?

_____

_____

_____

_____

_____

_____

_____

3. What do you need to continue to do that allows others to see your good works and glorify your Father in Heaven?

_____

_____

_____

_____

_____

_____

_____

_____

_____

_____

_____

_____

_____

_____

_____

_____

An Unforgettable Hug
from Charlie 'Tremendous' Jones

Don't just pretend to love others. Really love them.
Romans 12:9 (NLT)

I n 2008, an executive coaching client passed along a copy of my (Tim Enochs) book, *Every Day is Game Day*, to a man named Charlie "Tremendous" Jones. Within a few weeks, I was conversing via e-mail with Mr. Jones, discussing his thoughts about this little book I had written.

The relationship grew into telephone conversations. I was amazed by the wise counsel I received from such an influential person whom I had never met, but who gave his valuable time away to me so freely.

The relationship developed to the point that he invited my son and me to his home in Mechanicsburg, PA for a weekend. My son had never heard of Charlie 'Tremendous' Jones, but after hearing about the wisdom this man had shared with me, he became excited about the trip.

The time we were with this wonderful man will be embedded in our hearts forever. When we arrived at his home, he came out on the porch to greet us. After a congenial welcome, he opened his arms and gave us an unforgettable hug. Now, I'm a hugger and I've given and received many hugs in my life . . . but a hug from Charlie "Tremendous" Jones was unique. In fact, hugs from Charlie 'Tremendous' Jones were known and cherished by many people around the world.

You may be wondering, *who is this man?*

At the time my son and I went to Mechanicsburg, Charlie "Tremendous" Jones was one of the most influential people in the world. He had been recognized by the National Speakers Association as one of the top twenty speakers of the 20th century. His teaching, through seminars and books, had touched countless thousands of people around the world. One of his books had been translated into twelve languages with over 2,000,000 copies in print.

Charlie "Tremendous" Jones is frequently quoted, and you've probably heard his most famous quote: *"You will be the same person in five years as you are today except for the people you meet and the books you read."*

As you may imagine, we were very excited to hang out with someone with so much to share. On into the late evening, he imparted nugget after nugget of wisdom. There were several times that my son and I glanced over at each other in amazement. We were blessed to be there with him.

Nothing I have shared so far has indicated the state of Mr. Jones' health at the time of our visit. You see, he was so weak he could barely speak. He had to pause after almost every sentence to regain his breath. He was gallantly fighting a battle with cancer. Yet, he wanted to devote every ounce of strength he had to benefit others—right up to the end of his life. On the day we left, the head of Fox Entertainment was scheduled to arrive for a visit with Charlie 'Tremendous' Jones.

Charlie "Tremendous" Jones gave himself away, one breath at a time.

He didn't pretend to love people, he really loved them.

People who are on their way back to better don't just go through the motions and pretend to love other people . . . they truly love them.

Note: At 4:00 p.m., October 16, 2008, Charles Edward "Tremendous" Jones, with family at his side, triumphantly entered the gates of Heaven. We can only imagine the joy that he experienced! I still have Mr. Jones' cell number in my contacts on my cell and I have no plans to delete it!

Prayer
Heavenly Father, help me to really love people.

Think/Act
There are some people who are hard to like. The question here has to do with love. Are you really loving people? How did the story about Charlie "Tremendous" Jones impact you? Do you want to feel that kind of love from other people? Are you giving that kind of love to other people? It's easier to get caught up in everything going on in your life than to focus on love. But there is nothing better to do than love God with all of your heart, and

to love your neighbor as yourself. There is a reason this commandment is written many times in scripture.

Write about a time you felt real love from another person. How did that make you feel? What is one thing you can do to show that kind of love to someone else? When will you take that action?

_____

_____

_____

_____

_____

_____

_____

_____

_____

_____

_____

_____

_____

_____

When They Make It to My Floor

I must work the works of Him who sent Me while it is
day; the night is coming when no one can work.
John 9:4

Bubba had been battling a stroke and congestive heart failure for over a year. Dialysis kept him in Georgia, but Bubba wanted to travel. With his wife, Cindy, Bubba longed to make it to Arkansas to go fishing with his old friend, Larry. Bubba and Larry had played high school football together many years ago and were still close friends.

After convincing his doctors to let him skip dialysis, Bubba and Cindy were on their way to Arkansas. This wasn't their first time making this trip. But, for whatever reason, each time Bubba had made the statement that it might be his last. The trip in May of 2010 indeed was his last.

After returning home to Georgia, Bubba's health diminished rapidly. The physicians agreed to discontinue dialysis altogether, and Bubba was admitted into the hospital. Now it was Larry's turn to make the eight-hour drive from Arkansas to be with his friend, Bubba, in Georgia.

At some point during the second night of Bubba's hospital stay, one of the nurses on rotation made the following statement to Larry . . .

When patients make it to my floor, they don't talk about the 'stuff' they have or what they have done. They just want their family and friends.

Bubba was different. He made time to go fishing with his friend, Larry, long before he was confined to his final hospital stay. He didn't wait until he was on that nurse's floor to act on what he knew was important in his life. He chose friends and family over "stuff" before it was too late.

Why can't we be more like Bubba?

Why do we wait until we are so near the end to realize what really matters in life?

Prayer

Jesus, please help me to understand the brevity of life, and with that understanding help me to value what truly matters most.

Think/Act

What do you value most in life? Do you live your life in such a way that others see the value you put on what you say you value most? If so, great! If not, what needs to change? What will you do?

_____

_____

_____

_____

_____

_____

_____

_____

_____

_____

_____

_____

_____

_____

_____

_____

_____

_____

Day 34
Canary in a Coal Mine

Son of man, I have made you a watchman over the house
of Israel. When you hear a word from My mouth, give
them a warning from Me.
Ezekiel 3:17 (HCSB)

"Canary in a Coalmine" is a phrase used by coalminers.

The canary was very important to the American heroes who labored in the early days of coal mining. You see, a singing canary in a coal mine meant the air quality was good. A dead canary signaled that evacuation was necessary.

For the tough and rugged coal miners, these delicate yellow birds were a lifeline.

The canary is highly sensitive to traces of methane and carbon monoxide. A canary that detected carbon monoxide would sway noticeably before falling off the perch.

If the canary was chirping and singing, the workers could carry on without fear. If not, the warning was heeded immediately.

Even today in election years, some states may be referred to as the "canary in the coal mine." This refers to a political climate in that state which may signal the beginning of changes at the national level.

The point is that whether you are working in a coal mine, watching the election process, or trying to go back to better, you need a canary that can warn you of trouble ahead.

Prayer

Lord, help me to be warned when needed, and help me to heed the warning.

Think/Act

Consider the following questions . . .

1. Do you have a canary or someone who can warn you if you get off track in your life or business? This could be an accountability partner, a friend, or a coach that will ask you the tough questions and help you to detect danger in the atmosphere.

_____

_____

_____

_____

_____

_____

2. Does this person know what to look for in terms of your life, career, or area of responsibility? If not, make sure they are clear on both your goals and your areas of weakness. They can only help you as much as you will let them.

_____

_____

_____

_____

_____

_____

3. If you don't have that person in your life, why not? This may be a good time to check your "Why."

_____

_____

_____

_____

_____

_____

Everyone faces challenges and goes through difficult and dangerous times. Without a canary, or someone to warn you, your first sign of trouble may come too late.

Day 35

Hearing Voices

Keep your heart with all diligence,
For out of it spring the issues of life.
Proverbs 4:23

When we consider the term *hearing voices*, we usually think of auditory hallucinations, schizophrenia, or psychosis. However, we all hear voices—they are not hallucinations, but real people in real conversation or real words on a written page. Throughout the day, we are constantly bombarded with messages that impact the way we think, work, and play.

In his book, *Good to Great in God's Eyes*, Chip Ingram shared information from a twelve year study by University of Tennessee professor, Dr. Jack Haskins. In that study, Dr. Haskins found that after being exposed to negativity for only 5 minutes per day, people exhibited the following characteristics:

1. They were more depressed than before
2. They believed the world was a negative place
3. They were less likely to help others

4. They began to believe what they heard would soon happen to them

The concept of GIGO comes to mind: "Garbage In, Garbage Out." Whatever you allow to be put into your mind will be processed and will affect how you live. Fill your head with garbage, and your actions will be equally undesirable.

For some reason, it seems most of us are drawn to negativity. Garbage is often a hefty part of our auditory diet. But if you want to go back to better, it is critical that you focus on things that are good.

Wouldn't it be much better to think of GIGO as "Great In, Great Out?"

In The Message, the writer paraphrases Philippians 4:8 as follows: "Summing it all up, friends, I'd say you'll do best by filling your minds and meditating on things true, noble, reputable, authentic, compelling, gracious—the best, not the worst; the beautiful, not the ugly; things to praise, not things to curse."

There are two ways information enters our minds:

1. Intentional: We read or listen to something on purpose
2. Inadvertent: We allow ourselves to be in an environment where we are exposed to something

Either way, the thoughts and ideas we surround ourselves with enter our minds and influence the way we live. I encourage you to pay close attention to your environment, as well as what you intentionally allow to enter into your mind.

Whatever goes in there will be manifest in your life. Let it be greatness, not garbage.

People on their way back to better guard their heart.

Prayer

Lord, help me to filter out every voice that doesn't come from You. Help me to distinguish between what You want me to hear, whether that be an encouragement or a warning, and help me to ignore all other voices.

Think/Act

Begin to think about every "voice" that you hear throughout the day. Coworkers, social media, television, friends, family members, etc. Think about the quality of information you are taking in. This isn't to say that bad news is poor quality of information or that good news is necessarily good quality information. There are both good and bad sources that will tell you both pleasant and unpleasant things. Make a habit of strongly considering the source of the information you are receiving. In that consideration, think about how you might filter out those "bad voices" and tune in more closely to those "good voices."

_____

_____

_____

_____

_____

Day 36

Decisional Delusion

I say this in order that no one may delude you with
plausible arguments.
Colossians 2:4 (ESV)

*A*t times, some of us make decisions based on something other than the truth. Let's call that *decisional
delusion*. The word delusion means *something that
is falsely or delusively believed or propagated*. Decisional delusion
points to action—or inaction—that originates from poor understanding or a lack of clear thinking. You might call it a false belief.
No matter what it's called, the end result is usually not good.

One day, during a layover in Minneapolis, an author walked
into a bookstore to browse the time away. Something caught
his eye that made him feel ill. He had been thinking about
writing a book titled *Thinking Inside the Box for a Change*, but
had procrastinated.

Decisional delusion convinced him that he could always
write it later.

The book that jumped off the shelf at him was titled *Thinking Inside the Box*. After flipping through the pages, he could

tell the content was completely different than what he had been thinking about writing, but it was still too late. He knew that the opportunity to grab people's attention with that title had passed.

He had missed an opportunity because of Decisional Delusion. He falsely believed that he could always write that book later . . . so he chose to do something different than write that book. He was wrong, and that opportunity was gone.

In the end, a decision to do something now—or to do it later—is either based on absolute truth or it has some components of delusion. As he mentioned in a blog article titled *Procrastination is Your Friend*, procrastination is neither good nor bad. It depends on what you do with it.

In this case, because of a false belief (decisional delusion), he had made a poor choice in where to invest his time. That poor choice didn't happen overnight. There was a time when he could have still written that book and gotten away with a little procrastination. However, he never knew when that window of time slipped away . . . not until he saw that book on the shelf.

By the way, he bought that book as a reminder to not let opportunities pass because of procrastination.

Prayer

Jesus, You said in Your Word that You are the Way, the Truth, and the Life. There is no truth apart from You. I pray that Your Holy Spirit guides me in all truth so that I may be consistently on the correct path. Help me to seek and know the truth in every situation so that I may never be driven off course. Help me to always hold to the truth no matter how inconvenient or even dangerous it may be. Help me to always value and know the truth, because that is how I will always value and know You.

Think/Act

Create a discipline of using truth rather than assumption as your primary filter by which you pass every decision, action, and thought. There will be plenty of times when you may not have all the truth available to you in that given moment. But do the best you can with all the information that you have. Always remember that there is an absolute truth, and there is a correct answer. When we keep this truth in the forefront of our minds, we will begin to train ourselves to seek for the correct answer, and we will be much less likely to make bad decisions based on faulty information. This isn't to say that you will always make the right decision 100% of the time but considering the alternative of never looking for the truth in a matter, this will put you in a much more favorable outcome most of the time.

_____

_____

_____

_____

_____

_____

Day 37
Looking for a Sign

Moreover, the Lord spoke again to Ahaz, saying,
"Ask a sign for yourself from the Lord your God;
ask it either in the depth or in the height above."
Isaiah 7:10–11

a young lady was in the midst of a tough time when she was surprised by a report from her doctor that she was expecting. At this point in her life, she didn't see it as a good surprise. In her opinion, everything in her life would be deeply impacted by this unplanned baby. She didn't know what to do or where to turn. She didn't like any of the options available to her.

What was she to do?

She did what many people do when facing an impossible choice. She asked for a sign.

It so happened that in the moment when this request was heavy on her heart, she was waiting in the drive-through at Chick-fil-A. She certainly didn't expect to see her sign right away, especially not in line at *America's Best Quick Service Restaurant*!

But there it was! She noticed a bumper sticker on the car in front of her that read:

"Choose Life."

Immediately, she felt that this was the sign she had been waiting for.

She kept the baby and became so happy to be a mom!

Many times, the sign we are looking for is right there in front of us, but we miss it if we aren't observant. The car with the bumper sticker was there the entire time she was in line, but she just didn't see it at first.

When you see the sign God placed for you to see, you'll know it's meant for you. It may confirm what you already know and believe deep in your heart or be a new revelation that leaves no doubt. Sometimes we need something external to draw the truth out of our confusion. Somehow, she already knew keeping the baby was the only right move to make. The sign just helped her see the truth more clearly.

Always look for the right path.

Prayer

Lord, I know that You are always with me. I know that You will never forsake me. But honestly, sometimes I feel like I'm alone. I know this isn't true, but I can't help but feel like I'm facing life with no guidance at all. Help me to be ever mindful that You are with me, guiding me, despite my unawareness. Help me to search for You and be open to those signs that You may offer in unlikely places.

Think/Act

Create a habit of looking for wisdom in all situations whether they be good or bad. Work to become a person who seeks for and finds wisdom in your surroundings. This will also increase your critical thinking skills. Approach each hardship with an expectation of finding a way through it rather than with an expectation that all hope is lost.

_____

_____

_____

_____

_____

_____

_____

_____

_____

_____

_____

_____

_____

Day 38

Expecting Twins

For we are His workmanship, created in Christ Jesus
for good works, which God prepared beforehand
that we should walk in them.
Ephesians 2:10

There are three questions that you should never ask a woman:

1. How old are you?
2. How much do you weigh?
3. Are you expecting?

Imagine running into someone you have not seen in a while and noticing that they appear to be "expecting." Before you can stop yourself, you've said it: *Are you expecting?*

Appalled, the lady replies, "Well, no . . . do I look like I am expecting?"

A speaker actually asked this dangerous question—and got that very response—while onstage at a recent event! You may be thinking a lot of not-so-nice things about the speaker right now, so let me tell you the rest of the story . . .

While speaking at the BabyFest event about a book titled: *The CHILD Game Plan*, the speaker asked a volunteer to come up on stage with him. By the way, he set the whole thing up. She already knew the question he was going to ask, although she clearly wasn't expecting.

He asked the question. The lady responded, "No, do I look like I am expecting?" He emphatically replied, "Yes, in fact, I believe you are . . . expecting twins."

The amazing part of the story is that until that moment, she didn't know she was expecting!

You see, we should all be expecting twins. The names of the twins are **Purpose and Promise**. Of course, the lady wasn't expecting twin babies, or even one for that matter. Yet, she like everyone else in the world should be expecting . . . **Purpose and Promise**.

The question is not do we have those twins inside us. We do! The question is, what will we do with these two amazing twins?

In the book, *Every Day is Game* Day, we find that *Purpose begins to come into focus at the point where desire intersects with potential.* Your purpose lies somewhere in the area where what you want to do (your desire) aligns with what you have the potential to do.

That certainly doesn't mean that *everything* you want to do, and have the potential to do, makes up your purpose. That could get you in trouble. However, your true purpose does lie within that area, and you have to discipline yourself to find it. In doing this, you must understand your WHY.

There is no doubt that when you identify your true purpose, you will have the potential to bring it to fruition. If you couldn't, what would be the purpose of having a purpose.

People who are on their way back to better are expecting! They expect to live out their purpose by leaning into and taking the greatest advantage of their potential in every area of life.

Prayer

Father, I know that my purpose comes from You, for You are my Creator and my Designer. Not only have You given me my purpose in life, but You have given Your promise that You will guide me in living out my purpose. Right now, I don't want to ask You for anything. I just want to say thank You. Thank You for loving me enough to give me a specific purpose in life. Thank You for giving me Your promise that if I remain in You, that You will remain in me and that I can accomplish all that You have set out for me to do without exception.

Think/Act

Begin by creating a list of all the things that you enjoy doing. It might be in your day-to-day job, hiking in the mountains, raising your kids, cycling, being a caregiver, or working to help people buy their first home. Whatever you enjoy doing, put it on the list and title it "List A." Now make a separate list of all the things that you are either already good at or could be good at with the proper practice and/or education. Again, this could be anything. Call this "List B." Now look at List A and List B side by side. Try to look for similarities between those two lists. You will probably notice several. As you begin to notice some similarities, write those things on a third list called "List C." With your new List C, begin to think about how each thing on this list can have a positive impact on you, your loved ones, and other people in the world. Somewhere in this list might just be the beginning stages of discovering your purpose. Congratulations! You have now gone further on the path to discovering your purpose than the majority of people in the world.

_____

_____

_____

_____

_____

_____

_____

_____

_____

_____

_____

_____

_____

Day 39

Study Possibilities

Jesus said to him, "If you can believe,
all things are possible to him who believes.
Mark 9:23

There is an old recording of Jim Rohn talking about building unshakable character.

He suggested that we study possibilities.

Consider this question:

"What one thing does every baby, child, and adult have in common?"

The answer? Potential!

Considering Jim Rohn's suggestion that we should study possibilities, take a minute and think about some of the possibilities available to everyone, from infant to adult.

What is possible once a baby learns to crawl? Walk? Run?

What is possible if your child really applies himself/herself at school?

What is possible concerning your finances? . . . level of fitness? . . . vocational effectiveness?

What is possible in your personal relationships?

The more we consider possibilities, the more apt we are to dream great dreams. The more we dream great dreams, the more apt we are to take great action to achieve those dreams.

It all starts with the consideration of what is possible. Is there something in your life that seems to be impossible, but really isn't when you think about it?

Prayer

Lord, help me to see what You see. Help me to believe that through You, the otherwise impossible is, in fact, possible. Help me to know the potential that You have placed in me and to understand that if You have given me that potential, You have given it to me for a reason and it's my job to discover my purpose and live out the calling You have given me to my fullest potential.

Think/Act

Considering the following 9 steps:

1. Grab your dictionary. (You will need the "old school" paper dictionary for this exercise.)
2. Find the word impossible in your dictionary . . .
   Draw a straight line between the "m" and the "p" so it looks like this . . . im|possible

Now, place an apostrophe (') between the "i" and "m"
so it looks like this . . . i'm|possible
Can you see what's happening?
You are changing what was once impossible into I'm
possible

3. Now, make a list of three to five of the most desired possibilities in your life. Is it to get out of debt? Lose weight? Gain weight? Restore a relationship?

4. Remember, this has everything to do with what you desire and not the degree to which you believe it is possible.

5. Pick one that is most important to you right now.

6. Ask yourself . . . *For this to be possible, what is the first thing I need to do?*

7. Commit . . . and do it.

8. What's next? Add that to your list

9. Commit . . . and do it.

10. Repeat steps 7 and 8 until you experience that possibility as a reality in your life. Can you do that? Do you believe?

_____

_____

_____

_____

_____

_____

The 10 Page Miracle

*Bring the cloak that I left with Carpus at Troas when you
come—and the books, especially the parchments.*
2 Timothy 4:13

We know from many direct references in the Epis-
tles, Paul was a diligent student and most likely
an avid reader. Even when he was nearing the
end of his life, of the many things he could have requested, he
wanted his books, especially the parchments.

During a seminar, the topic of reading came up and it was
clear that everyone in the room felt it was a worthy enterprise,
but few had recently cracked open the pages of a book. Hyrum
Smith, the presenter, said:

*You've obviously placed a value on reading, but you're not doing
it. Why aren't you doing it?*

One man in the back of the room raised his hand and said:

Because books don't ring.

As some people in the room wondered what the man meant
by that statement, he elaborated. When your telephone rings,
you normally stop what you're doing and answer the call, or at

least see who is calling. When the doorbell rings, you at least peek out the window to see who is at the door. When the alarm clock goes off in the morning, it's hard to sleep through it. Those and many other things get your attention and you take action.

However, when you set a book aside, it doesn't ring, or flash, or do anything to grab your attention again. So, no action is taken concerning the book. It just sits there on the table gathering dust, waiting for you to pick it up. Sadly, that happens with many people concerning reading the Bible. Books just sit there, quietly allowing you to go about your day. They do nothing to assert themselves into your routine.

There are times when a book may capture your attention to the extent that you can hardly put it down, but not all books worth reading are exciting or riveting. It takes discipline to read. This is the kind of discipline that Jim Rohn called "the bridge between thought and accomplishment."

Reading is a bridge that can close the gap between what you know and what you should know. People interested in self-development make reading a regular discipline.

If you aren't an avid reader and you need a little help with this discipline, consider the following: reading only 10 pages per day will allow you to read 3,650 pages each year. Here's why that simple discipline could be called *a miracle*.

The CHILD Game Plan is a book about developing a winning game plan for kids. It has 163 pages. By reading 10 pages per day, you could read 22 books that length per year.

When was the last time you read 22 books in a year?

War and Peace contains 1296 pages. It's a thick book! Reading 10 pages each day would allow you to completely read through that book almost 3 times in a year! Not that you'd want to, but you get the point.

Now, could you commit to reading 10 pages per day over the next 90 days? If you make that commitment, and stick to it, you will read 900 pages, or just over 4 average length books over the next 90 days.

There's a wealth of information and ideas out there, and you have a choice. You can let that valuable information collect dust or you can turn the ringer off your phone and pick up a book. Develop the discipline of reading, and it will enrich your life and career for many years to come.

Will you commit to reading 10 pages a day for the next 90 days?

Prayer

Father, You have offered us a wealth of knowledge in our world. Though there is no source of wisdom that is as pure and divinely inspired as Your Word, You have gifted many men and women with the capability to compile and produce works that would be for our benefit if we would simply take the time to dig. All wisdom and knowledge come from You. Help me to seek it out. Help me to hunger for it. Help me to place a high value on attaining and sharing wisdom from You.

Think/Act

As you read above, create a discipline of reading (or listening) to something on a frequent basis. A good way to do this is by setting for yourself a bite-size goal of reading ten pages a day (or even ten pages five days a week). Once you develop this habit, it will become easier and easier to maintain this discipline and you will be allowing yourself to gain access to so much more wisdom than you ever dreamed. Granted, there are many sources that are not worth learning from, but developing a discipline of reading will also allow you to learn which sources are a rich mine of gold, and which sources are not worth your time.

_____

_____

_____

_____

_____

_____

_____

_____

_____

_____

_____

_____

_____

_____

_____

Mailbox Baseball

But even if you suffer for doing what is right,
God will reward you for it.
1 Peter 3:14a (NLT)

While driving, have you ever noticed a large dent on one side of a mailbox along the road?

If so, you may be able to guess how it got there. Hint, it probably wasn't hit by a bird. These beat up mailboxes were usually the result of a game called Mailbox Baseball. Mailbox Baseball is played by a passenger in a moving vehicle, hitting the side of a mailbox with a baseball bat. This *game* results in the destruction of the mailbox, which is a federal crime. Intentionally damaging a mailbox is punishable by fine and up to three years in prison. Certainly not the kind of game you want to win, lose, or even play!

If it's happened to you, you probably have questions. Who could have done this? Why my mailbox? Why weren't other mailboxes in my neighborhood damaged like this? What will I do if I discover who did it? Should I report them? Should I demand that they, or their parents (assuming it was a minor), pay for a replacement? All sorts of questions would probably be swirling through your head.

Here's a true story of mailbox baseball . . .

Upon arriving home, I noticed my mailbox had a severe dent on one side. I just knew it was the result of mailbox baseball. I am going to discover who did it, and they will pay. Irritated, I strode to the damaged box to retrieve the mail. Lying there, on top of my "official" mail, was a handwritten note that had clearly not been delivered by the USPS.

To whom it may concern,

I am very sorry that I accidently damaged your mailbox. I will be happy to pay for the damages. My cell phone number is (###-####).

The lady who hit the mailbox had also signed the note.

All of a sudden, my irritation turned to compassion for someone who could be so honest and concerned about the damage done to my box.

I called the number and spoke with this woman, a young mother who had been parked on my street while she was working for my neighbor. Upon getting a call from her son's school, she needed to leave immediately to pick him up. As she was leaving, she inadvertently hit our mailbox.

I could picture this young mother, already stressed over the call about her son, staring at the damaged mailbox. Her day had just gone from bad to worse. I've had days like that myself.

I told her not to worry about the mailbox.

I also commended her for leaving the note. She could have left the scene and I would have never known what happened. She told me that, although she was somewhat afraid to do so, leaving the note was the right thing to do.

I realized that there was a very important lesson to be learned as well as a very important question I had to ask myself.

The Lesson:

Assumptions can lead us down the wrong path . . . always get the facts first.

The Question:

What would I have done in her situation?

She was in a hurry, yet she stopped to do the right thing. She was afraid, yet she overrode her fear to do the right thing. She could have gotten away with it, yet she faced the consequences and did the right thing.

She could have driven off . . . and you would be reading something else for Day 41.

Yet, because she wrote the note, we know she made the right decision that day.

Prayer

Lord, help me to never make assumptions without knowing all the relevant facts. Help me to be quick to forgive and slow to anger. Help me to begin with a posture of compassion. Teach me what it means to love the way that you love and to value mercy over judgment.

Think/Act

Next time you are faced with a situation where you are angry, take some time and think about all the possible responses you could give. Think about the response you would give in your anger. Think about the repercussions of that response. Think about the response you could give once you have had time to cool off. Consider all the facts and then make a sober minded decision rather than an emotional reaction. What are the possible outcomes of the sober minded decision? Now, which outcome do you prefer? Which outcome would you prefer if it were you who were the offender?

_____

_____

_____

_____

_____

_____

_____

_____

Day 42

Who Needs a Second Chance?

. . . for all have sinned and fall short of the glory of God
Romans 3:23

*H*ave you ever needed a second or third chance in some area of life? Or have you ever given someone a second or third chance to get things turned around? Whether you like football or any sport at all, the Jeremiah Masoli story of second and third chances is inspiring!

At the University of Oregon, anticipation was high prior to the 2009 football season. Among other weapons in the Ducks' arsenal, they had one of the top quarterbacks in the nation, Jeremiah Masoli.

The Ducks did not disappoint. With Masoli at the helm of a dynamic offense, the Ducks gave their fans an exciting season. They finished at the top of the Pac 10 Conference and earned a spot in the Rose Bowl. Masoli was mentioned in some circles as a Heisman Trophy candidate.

He was a high-profile quarterback with a bright future ahead.

When you are a promising young athlete, the spotlight is always on you. High profile college football players are usually a great topic for discussion on sports shows, blogs, and magazine articles. Everything they do, good and bad, is documented and shared with the world. Sometimes the good and the bad can be blown out of proportion to the extent that these eighteen- to twenty-year-old young athletes appear to be better—or worse—than they really are. Sometimes it just isn't fair.

Coming off of such an amazing year, and with another year ahead to further establish his prowess as a quarterback, Masoli should have been guarding his future carefully. So, imagine the shock and disappointment felt by Oregon fans when he was arrested and pled guilty to charges of misdemeanor burglary.

Oregon Head Coach (at that time) Chip Kelly made the decision to suspend him for the season with the opportunity to play again the following year. It was an offer of a second chance which Masoli accepted.

Then, it happened again. In June, Masoli was charged with possession of less than an ounce of marijuana. He had failed to live up to his bargain with his Coach. Kelly immediately dismissed him from the team.

Jeremiah Masoli did some things that, in his words, *let a lot of people down*, including himself. For all his talent, he found himself a homeless athlete—a star quarterback without a team. However, in Coach Kelly's words: *He's made some bad decisions, but he's not a bad kid.*

Masoli was given a third chance. He enrolled at Ole Miss as a walk-on quarterback for the Rebels. Masoli was clearly grateful: *I am very excited about this opportunity and very thankful Ole Miss is giving me this chance.*

Fast forward . . . Masoli played for Ole Miss and earned the opportunity to play pro football. In 2018, he was recognized as the East Division's Most Outstanding Player in the Canadian Football League. In July of 2019, he experienced a season-ending knee injury. Although knee injuries can be career ending, the Hamilton Tiger-Cats re-signed him for 2020. Needless to say, Jeremiah Masoli has made the most out of an additional chance given to him.

Here's what the Tiger-Cats' head coach, Orlondo Steinauer, had to say about re-signing Masoli:

> It's exciting to have Jeremiah back for the 2020 season. His high character, remarkable work ethic and competitiveness make him a natural fit for our organization.

Not bad for a thirty-one-year-old professional quarterback coming off a major injury!

Student athletes are still so young, and yet we expect them to succeed in superhuman ways amid a ton of pressure. That pressure certainly doesn't justify bad decisions, but it does make for an uphill battle.

You and I may not be subject to the scrutiny of the masses, but we all are under some degree of pressure to succeed. And because we're human, we are bound to disappoint now and then. Surely there have been times when we've all needed a second, third, or fourth chance to "get it right." Jeremiah accepted the opportunity and turned things around for himself.

Prayer

Lord, I can't thank you enough for loving me beyond my first, second, or my one thousandth failure. Thank you for giving me chance after undeserved chance to walk in the calling that you have set before me. Help me to never lose sight of what you have called me to do. Help me to never take your grace for granted and keep my mind focused and my heart grounded.

Think/Act

An old African adage suggests, "look not to where you fell, but to where you first stumbled." Many times, we focus on where the failure actually happened rather than on what led to the failure. Be vigilant in the things you should prevent from happening. You may have heard that prevention is better than cure. This is a proactive approach rather than a reactive one.

_____

_____

_____

_____

_____

_____

_____

_____

More Blessed to Give

Give, and it will be given to you: good measure,
pressed down, shaken together and running over will be
put into your bosom. For with the same measure
that you use, it will be measured back to you.
Luke 6:38

One young man had a conversation with his dad that changed the young man's life. It went like this . . .

Hey dad, I believe everything in the Bible, but there is one part I really have trouble with . . .

What's that son?

How can it be more blessed to give than to receive? I guess it's ok to give stuff away, but I really feel more blessed when I get stuff. At Christmas, it's good to give presents, but I really enjoy being on the receiving side. So, I would think it's more blessed to get stuff than to give it away. Can you help me understand?

In his wisdom, his dad answered his son with a question.

Would you rather be on the side of needing someone to give something to you, or would you rather be living in a season of abundance and be willing to give to someone else in need?

The young man quickly realized he had it all upside down. He thought receiving was a blessing that led to a life of abundance and all the "good stuff" that goes with it. When, in reality, giving leads to abundance, and all the "good" that goes with it. *Notice, what's missing in that statement is the word,* **stuff***.*

You see, there is joy in giving; and everyone can give something.

Maybe it's not money, maybe it's not "stuff," but everyone has something to give.

You can give a smile . . .

think about how you feel when someone smiles at you.

You can give a kind word . . .

". . . the right word at the right time is like precious gold set in silver (Proverbs 25:11).

You can give your time . . .

nothing is more valuable than your time.

The benefits of giving go well beyond the moment. After the conversation with his dad, the young man remembered that when he was younger, he and his family had visited his uncle at an Army base where they met one of his uncle's friends. As they were sitting near the commissary, he mentioned that he was hungry. His uncle's friend immediately jumped up and ordered a burger for him. Of course, he wasn't starving, but young boys are always hungry. His spontaneous kindness touched the boy's heart. He said he has never forgotten that moment. In fact, along with the conversation with his dad, God used that friend's kindness to shape his understanding of generosity.

Prayer

Father, give me a heart that is generous with all that You have given me. Help me to realize that my possessions, my relationships, my talents, my energy, and my time are gifts from You. They are given for me to be a good steward and to give generously from my abundance.

Think/Act

Think about everything you have: time, talent, energy, recourses. What are you doing with all of these things? Are you hoarding them so that you can retain the excess for yourself? Are you giving of your time, talent, energy, and resources so that others may be blessed by them as you have been?

_____

_____

_____

_____

_____

_____

_____

_____

_____

_____

_____

_____

_____

_____

_____

_____

_____

_____

Corn Grows, Weeds Grow, and Life Slips Away

*I went past the field of a sluggard, past the
vineyard of someone who has no sense; thorn
had come up everywhere, the ground was covered
with weeds, and the stone wall was in ruins.*
Proverbs 24:30–31 (NIV)

*H*ave you ever been driving on a country road and noticed tall corn growing in a field just before harvest? Sometimes it seems as if the corn stalks just shoot up overnight. Maybe it's a corn field you have driven by every day but just haven't noticed how tall the corn had grown until that one day, and there it is, beautiful tall healthy stalks of corn!

Of course, your lack of attention to the corn as you drove by the field everyday didn't hinder its growth at all. It just kept growing.

There is a natural process that causes corn to grow. It begins with planting and continues until harvest. It starts with a seed that absorbs nutrients and moisture from the ground. The sun does its part, and within a few weeks, a corn stalk can grow up to 15 feet tall.

This happens because it is following the course of nature.

There are physical laws at work to make the corn grow.

Corn is good. It is high in fiber, vitamins B1, B5, and C, and is rich in folate which helps the generation of new cells. Not to mention, it's delicious with melted butter and a dash of salt. The physical laws that make corn grow work together for my benefit.

However, those same laws can work against the farmer and all of us.

Just as you can drive past a cornfield and not notice how the corn is growing, it's possible to not notice weeds growing around shrubs planted near your house or the house of your neighbor. Lack of attention to the weeds didn't stunt their growth either. They just followed their natural course and grew.

The same natural laws that were working to the farmer and consumer's benefit with corn can work against a homeowner concerning weeds.

Here's a question. Could you and I be missing the growth of weeds in our own lives?

Bad habits can take root and germinate when we're not paying attention. Neglected problems in our work can gradually drain our resources and energy.

What about the good healthy things in life?

Are we paying enough attention to them? If you are a parent, you might be missing the opportunity to watch your kids grow. We all could be overlooking opportunities to strengthen relationships.

The good news is that if we are vigilant and take care of what matters most, over time we can grow more of the good things in life. It's just a natural law to understand that corn grows, weeds grow, and life can slip away before we know it.

Prayer

Lord, help me to notice those things in my life that I might be overlooking or ignoring. Help me to shift my focus on those weeds that need to be pulled and those good crops that need to continue to grow. Give me a heart of discernment that I might know where to focus my effort and keep a mind, body, and spirit that glorifies you.

Think/Act

It's easy to ignore or overlook those things in life that we wish would just go away. The sad news is if you ignore them, they don't go away, they grow bigger. Consider those things that you may have been ignoring for a while, your health, your finances, and addiction, etc. What are some of the weeds that are sprouting up that have the potential to choke out the good things that God has planted in your life? Write down as many of those things that you can think of and make an action plan on how to remove those weeds from your life.

_____

_____

_____

_____

_____

Day 45
How Will You Be Remembered

I thank my God upon every remembrance of you
Philippians 1:3

Imagine getting a letter like the one below, shortly after your spouse's death:

I am sorry to learn of the death of your husband, Alex. During the 17 years he worked here, Alex was a valued and dedicated employee and we appreciate his contributions to the company.

My sympathy to you, and the other members of your family in your loss.

The note was written and signed by the CEO of the company where Alex worked. What an expression of gratitude!

Now for the surprising part of the story: At the time of his passing, Alex had been gone from this company for over ten years!

Think back to where you were ten years ago. How do you think you would be remembered by those people? How do you remember them?

Perhaps there is someone you knew ten years (or 10 days) ago who needs to hear of your gratitude today.

Now, consider where you are today. How will you be remembered 10 years from now?

The lady who shared this letter was Alex's daughter. She was elated to read that letter about her dad. It is our hope that her willingness to allow us to share this letter with you will cause you to think about your past contributions, and more importantly, that we will all live today in such a way that we will be worthy of our family receiving a letter like that someday.

Prayer

Father, guide my life so that when others think of me, they see the love and nature of Jesus. Help me to always imitate Him in all that I do so that others will remember more of Him and less of me.

Think/Act

This may be the toughest thing you've had to do during these 49 days. Write your own eulogy. You read that right. Take some time and think about what you hope others would say about you once you're gone. Now consider if the life you are currently living would match up to what you hope others say about you. What, if anything, needs to change about your life now in order to make people's memory of you match what you hope they would say?

_____

_____

_____

_____

_____

_____

_____

_____

_____

_____

_____

_____

_____

_____

_____

_____

_____

_____

Day 46
Walking Her Home

Let your light so shine before men, that they may see your
good works and glorify your Father in Heaven.
Matthew 5:16

In his song *Walking Her Home,* Mark Schultz tells the
story of Henry and Liz. In the liner notes of Wow Hits
2008, he says:

Henry and Liz were my neighbors when I first moved
to Nashville. Henry told me that on their first date
her father said, 'Son, take good care of my daughter. Walk her home from the movies and promise me
you'll never leave her side.' A couple of years ago I visited them in a nursing home. After a hug and saying
goodbye, I stood at the front door and watched them
walk down the hall, arm in arm. Henry was walking
her back to her room. I remembered the promise that
he made to her father, to walk her home and never
leave her side . . . He was still doing it.

Consider your life. Are you committed to living out what you have planned? Do you have a written Life Plan? If you do, when was the most recent time you read it? When was it most recently updated?

The world is full of great stories. Live your life today so that your story is an example for others to follow, not a warning for others to avoid.

Prayer

Father, help me to never forget that it is You who has ordered my steps. Help me to view my entire life as being in service to You. Physical, Emotional, Intellectual, Relational, Vocational, Financial, Recreational, and Spiritual, every area of my life belongs completely to You. Guide me as I navigate my life through its joys and challenges. Help me to live a full life in the way that you have set out for me. Help me to take every path You have prepared for me and to avoid every path that will lead me away from You.

Think/Act

Consider the eight areas of your life, physical, emotional, intellectual, relational, vocational, financial, recreational, and spiritual. Which of these areas need the most work? In what ways can you alter the current course of your life in one or more of these areas? How can these changes lead you closer to a fulfilled life that gives glory to God?

_____

_____

_____

_____

_____

_____

_____

_____

_____

_____

_____

_____

_____

_____

_____

_____

_____

_____

_____

_____

Day 47
Hold on to Your Fork

Let us hold fast the confession of our hope without
wavering, for He who promised is faithful.
Hebrews 10:23

There is a story about an elderly lady named Sally who had an unusual request.

She was meeting with the man she had asked to deliver the message at her funeral. She had picked out the songs, selected the casket in which she wanted to be buried, as well as the final clothing she would wear.

Bill, there is one more thing I want you to do for me when I die.

What's that Sally?

I want to be buried with a fork in my hand.

A fork?

Yes, a fork. You see, every Thanksgiving my grandmother always cooked a great meal for us. Her table was filled with ham, turkey, dressing, and everything else that goes with it. After we finished the meal, as she was collecting the plates, she always leaned over and whispered, 'Hold on to your fork honey, you are going to need it.' I knew this meant I was about to get a piece of her famous chocolate pie.

I want to be buried holding on to a fork because I believe something better is on the way. And I want to remind others that the best is yet to come.

Do you believe there is something better coming in your life? Sally's grandmother gave her hope by telling her to hold on to her fork. Do you have something or someone that reminds you to hope? It is important to have hope and give hope to others.

In my book, *The Speed of Favor*, I (Tim Hill) shared how *I came to understand by the Spirit, which was confirmed by the Word of God, that as sure as there is a speed of light and a speed of sound, there is a speed of favor—a divine pace at which God sovereignly pours out His blessings upon us.* Hold on to your fork. The answer you need, the blessing you desire, and the hope you may desperately want to see restored just may be coming at you at God's faster than light Speed of Favor.

Prayer

Lord, I just want to thank You that this life, with all of its joys and challenges, is not all that You have to offer me. I want to thank You for offering salvation to me and for the promise that comes after this life. Thank You for the glorious resurrection that You have promised for all those who have faith in Your Son, Jesus. Thank You for the wonderful life that You have prepared for all those who love You. Help me, oh God, to never forget that the best of this life pales in comparison to the glory that awaits us in the next life.

Think/Act

Take some time today to think about all the good that's been in your life. Sadly, for some this list may be shorter than others. Regardless, if it's from your childhood, from a moment with a friend, or when you held your child for the first time, think about that fleeting moment of pure bliss. Your fondest memory on this earth can't even compare to what awaits everyone who has put their faith in Jesus. Use this as an encouragement that will propel you forward past any opposition, whether it be internal or external. Always look forward to what's awaiting you as you diligently work hard to complete the tasks God has given you now.

Day 48

Keep on Keeping On

Then he said, 'Take the arrows'; so, he took them.
And he said to the king of Israel, 'Strike the ground';
so, he struck three times, and stopped. And the man
of God was angry with him, and said, 'You should have
struck five or six times; then you would have struck
Syria till you had destroyed it! But now you
will strike Syria only three times.'
2 Kings 13:18–19

Why was Elisha angry? Joash, the king of Israel, came to Elisha and wept over his concern for the nation. Elisha told Joash to get a bow and some arrows. Then he told Joash to take the bow in his hand, open the east window and shoot. He did. Elisha then told Joash to take the arrows and strike the ground. Joash struck the ground 3 times and stopped. Elisha was angry because he stopped too soon. Have you ever stopped too soon?

Vince Lombardi is known as one of the greatest football coaches in history. He said: *What I believe is, that if you go out on the football field on Sunday or any other endeavor in life and you leave every fiber of what you have on that field when the game finally ends, then you've won.*

Joash only struck the ground three times. Elisha said: *. . . you should have struck five or six times . . .* He didn't leave every fiber of what he had on the field, whether it was arrows striking the ground or effort. Therefore, he limited his victory to the number of times he struck the ground.

There's an old phrase: **Keep on keeping on.** Don't quit because you feel like quitting or because current circumstances are getting you down. You can find a way to go on.

Pick up your dreams and goals, dust them off, get back in the game, and keep on keeping on until the complete victory is won!

Prayer

Lord, everything I have, my talents, my purpose, and my very breath is from You. Help me to hold nothing back in my pursuit of accomplishing the tasks You have given me. Help me to offer it all in service to You.

Think/Act

What are those things that you tend to keep back from devoting to God? What do you tend to reserve for yourself? Maybe you have offered everything else in your life, but there's one area you just can't seem to let go. Is it because you're embarrassed? Is it because you feel like you're unqualified? When you close your eyes for the last time in this life (hopefully a very long time from now), will you feel confident that you used everything God gave you in service back to Him? Explore the deep recesses of your heart and consider what you may have yet to offer God.

_____

_____

_____

_____

_____

_____

_____

_____

_____

_____

_____

_____

_____

_____

_____

_____

_____

_____

_____

_____

Day 49
March On!

See! I have given Jericho into your hand, its king, and the mighty men of valor.
Joshua 6:2

There are times when you experience instant victory and times when it takes a little more work and steadfast faith. While we all prefer instant victory, or even victory before the battle starts, there are times when the greater victory comes after persistent prayer and obedience.

My (Tim Hill) dad, John Hill, preached 5,100 sermons in his lifetime. One of those sermons was titled: ***Have You Stopped Marching Around Your Walls?*** In this sermon, he shared the story of Joshua and the walls of Jericho from Joshua Chapter 6.

For a fleeting moment, Joshua may have thought the gates would open and white flags of surrender would welcome him and his army in to take over the city. But God followed that prophetic verse with something for Joshua and his army to do first.

In Joshua 6:3–5, God said:

You shall march around the city, all you men of war; you shall go all around the city once. This you shall do six days. And seven priests shall bear seven trumpets of rams' horns before the ark. But the seventh day you shall march around the city seven times, and the priests shall blow the trumpets. It shall come to pass, when they make a long blast with the ram's horn, and when you hear the sound of the trumpet, that all the people shall shout with a great shout; then the wall of the city will fall down flat. And the people shall go up every man straight before him.

From John Hill's sermon:

Not every wall falls down the first time you march around it. Not every game is won in the third inning, the sixth, or the ninth. The issue is that too many people quit too soon.

There is no substitute for the daily march. Most of Israel quit too soon . . .

There will be a moment for shouting. But right now, God wants you to march around the wall . . . Will you stay at the job until the victory comes? There may be some weary footsteps to plod before the walls (or your Jericho) fall down.

There were no cracks in the wall after the first day. There were no cracks in the wall after the seventh march around Jericho on the seventh day because God had said: *It shall come to pass, when they make a long blast* with the ram's horn, *and* when you hear the sound of the trumpet, that all the people shall shout with a great shout; then the wall of the city will fall down flat. . . .

Keep marching until God says it is time to shout!

Prayer

Father don't let me forget that it is You who leads and guides me. Let me never forget that if You have called me, it is only You who can stop me. Help me to never quit, never to let up, and never be lax in the pursuit of completing the tasks that You have given me.

Think/Act

Whatever you feel your calling is in life, think about who or what is at stake if you give up. Write down the names and groups of people who will be at a loss if you allow yourself to stop. Review this list whenever you feel overwhelmed, bogged down, or defeated. Think about these people. Think about the impact that God has called you to have on their life and keep going!

Final Note

*I*n this season, many people are looking forward to getting back to normal. Some are talking about a new normal. However, many are referring to a "normal" defined by someone else. You can be different. Ask God how He wants you to go back to BETTER. Let God define your new "normal" as BETTER.

We believe God has great things planned for you!

About the Authors

*D*r. **Tim Hill** has served in national and international Christian leadership for many years. As general overseer of the Church of God (Cleveland, TN), he serves as presiding bishop for over seven million members of the church in over 180 countries around the world. His past service as general director of World Missions for the Church of God (Cleveland, TN) took him to more than 100 nations of the world, giving oversight to a large multifaceted and diverse global ministry. Previous ministry roles include assistant general overseer and secretary general of the Church of God; chairman of the Church of God International Executive Council; and as administrative bishop of the Church of God in Southern Ohio and Oklahoma. Prior to entering administrative work, Dr. Hill served as senior pastor of River Oak Church of God in Danville, Virginia, where he hosted daily television and radio programs. He is a graduate of Lee University in Cleveland, Tennessee and received a Doctorate of Ministry from Church of God Theological Seminary, Cleveland, Tennessee. Dr. Hill has authored several books of sermons and has written 200 gospel songs. He is the author of the number one song, "He's Still in the Fire," which was voted Song of the Year by *Gospel Voice* Magazine. He began recording at age sixteen and has eighteen recording projects to his credit, including many original songs. Traveling extensively worldwide, Dr. Hill speaks in major denominational and interdenominational conventions and conferences.

Tim Enochs has been an executive coach for over twenty years, coaching leaders, executives, and company owners to discover or rediscover their purpose and vision in life and work, then live it out in a balanced way that produces irrefutable success in every endeavor. Prior to that, Tim had extensive experience in human resources in a wide range of organizations, spanning from manufacturing to banking. In addition to being an executive coach, Tim is a co-founder of NEWLife Leadership and the *New York Times* best-selling author of *On The Clock*, executive producer of the movie *Welcome to Inspiration* (based on his book, *The Street Sweeper*), and author of five other books, including *Uncommon Influence*, *The CHILD Game Plan*, *The Foundation*, *The 7 Revelations for Irrefutable Success*, and *Every Day is GameDay*. Tim is also a highly-rated national/international speaker. He received his Bachelor of Business Administration in Management from Ole Miss and his MBA from The University of Tennessee–Martin.

Adam Enochs is an executive coach, co-founder of NEWLife Leadership, and the leadership development manager for First Citizens National Bank in Tennessee. Adam has extensive leadership experience with Chick-fil-A and is also co-developer of the NEWLife Leadership Coach Certification Program. He received his Bachelor of Science in Business as well as his Masters of Leadership from Lee University in Cleveland, TN.

A free ebook edition is available with the purchase of this book.

To claim your free ebook edition:

1. Visit MorganJamesBOGO.com
2. Sign your name CLEARLY in the space
3. Complete the form and submit a photo of the entire copyright page
4. You or your friend can download the ebook to your preferred device

Print & Digital Together Forever.

Snap a photo

Free ebook

Read anywhere